D1050269

MY  WORLD

4-03

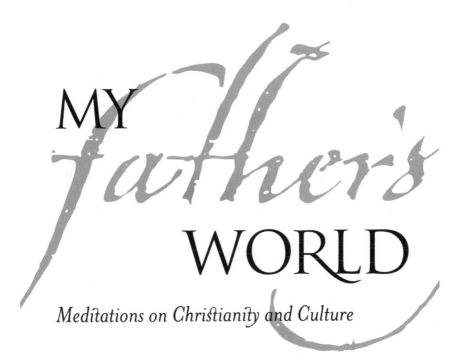

MY *father's* WORLD

Meditations on Christianity and Culture

Philip Graham Ryken

FOREWORD BY C. EVERETT KOOP

P&R PUBLISHING

P.O. BOX 817 • PHILLIPSBURG • NEW JERSEY 08865-0817

© 2002 by Philip Graham Ryken

All rights reserved. No part of this book may be reproduced, stored in a retrieval system, or transmitted in any form or by any means—electronic, mechanical, photocopy, recording, or otherwise—except for brief quotations for the purpose of review or comment, without the prior permission of the publisher, P&R Publishing Company, P.O. Box 817, Phillipsburg, New Jersey 08865-0817.

Unless otherwise indicated, Scripture quotations are from the HOLY BIBLE, NEW IN-TERNATIONAL VERSION®. NIV®. Copyright © 1973, 1978, 1984 by International Bible Society. Used by permission of Zondervan Publishing House. All rights reserved.

Scripture quotations marked NKJV are from The Holy Bible, New King James Version. Copyright © 1979, 1980, 1982, Thomas Nelson, Inc.

Scripture quotations marked KJV are from the King James Version of the Bible.

Scripture quotations marked NASB are from the NEW AMERICAN STANDARD BIBLE®. ©Copyright The Lockman Foundation 1960, 1962, 1963, 1968, 1971, 1972, 1973, 1975, 1977. Used by permission.

Italics in Scripture quotations indicate emphasis added.

Page design by Tobias Design
Typesetting by Michelle Feaster

Printed in the United States of America

Library of Congress Cataloging-in-Publication Data

Ryken, Philip Graham, 1966–
    My Father's world : meditations on Christianity and culture /
Philip Graham Ryken.
        p. cm.
    Includes bibliographical references (p.) and indexes.
    ISBN 0-87552-560-1 (pbk.)
    I. Title

BR115.C8 .R95 2002
261—dc21

2002023870

To
Miss Killip, Miss Hiatt, Miss Himmel, Miss Bingham,
and the other fine teachers at the Wheaton Christian Grammar School
who helped me look at the world like a child of God.

"The fear of the Lord is the beginning of knowledge." (Prov. 1:7a)

Wherever man may stand, whatever he may do, to whatever he may apply his hand, in agriculture, in commerce, and in industry, or his mind, in the world of art, and science, he is, in whatsoever it may be, constantly standing before the face of his God, he is employed in the service of his God, he has strictly to obey his God, and above all, he has to aim at the glory of his God.

—ABRAHAM KUYPER

CONTENTS

Part 3 Love, Marriage, and Family

Part 4 The Arts

Part 5 Science and Technology

CONTENTS

CONTENTS

FOREWORD

While Surgeon General of the United States, I was awarded the Jefferson medal. During the ceremony, the presenter referred to a recent profile of me in the *Washington Post* titled "The Unpredictable Surgeon General."

The ceremony calls for three individuals who know the recipient well to make comment in the spirit of the occasion. One commentator was Dr. Tony Fauci, one of my Commissioned Officers, an assistant Surgeon General, my personal physician, and a treasured friend. "Unpredictable?" Tony began. "Chick Koop is the most predictable man in Washington. Tell me what dilemma you'll present to him next year, and I'll give you his response!"

But only God is totally predictable: "Jesus Christ is the same yesterday and today, yes and forever" (Heb. 13:8 NASB). I have always thought of God as having a personality. Though the Bible says, "His ways are past finding out," I believe that the more one learns about God the more predictable he becomes. When faith is necessary, it is his gift to us. When grace is poured out, it is done so abundantly, "more than one could ask or think."

God is in everything. One paradox of the relationship between the Creator and his creatures is how much easier it is for the child raised in its natural surroundings to see God in the rising of the sun than it is for the affluent city-dweller to see him in an illuminated light bulb. The inhabitant of a primitive culture finds in the almost indescribably complex anatomy and function of the human hand, not the God of evolution, but the God of creation: "By faith we understand that the worlds were prepared by the word of God, so that what is seen was not made out of things which are visible" (Heb. 11:3 NASB).

The primitive creature and the most learned can both affirm with Isaac Newton: "In the absence of any other proof, the thumb alone would convince me of the existence of God."

Analogies to God break down because we are dealing with a "personality." Though Jesus was fully man, he was a sinless, holy man. We may be unable to predict what he would eat, but we know that the sin of individuals and nations will be judged according to his righteousness.

Philip Ryken has written a series of brief essays of pleasing and beneficial variety. One cannot escape the fact that God is in *Christians in the World* just as he is in *The Bible*; in *Love, Marriage, and the Family* as he is in *The Arts*; and in *Science and Technology* as he is in *Social Issues*—each of these titles a section in the collection. And because all the essays come under the rubric of *My Father's World*, the same God connected to "Homo Sapiens for Sale" is encountered in "Why Humans Have Rights."

More than a series of essays, *My Father's World* is a series of encounters with the God who made the end when he made the beginning, connected together to teach us about the character and "personality" of God.

Read on. Bask in the sovereignty of God. Know this serendipity by the way he works in the world and our lives. If perhaps you don't yet know him, he just may introduce himself to you.

C. Everett Koop, M.D., Sc.D.

INTRODUCTION

*W*e are all theologians. Theology is the study of God and his relationship to the world. Since we all have beliefs about God and since we
all live in his world, we are all theologians. Even atheists are theologians—
they just aren't very good ones. They begin with the belief that there is no
God, and everything else follows. But even in their rejection of God they
are thinking from a theological point of view.

Whether you realize it or not you too are a theologian. And if that is
true, then you should try to become a good one. This is part of my mission
in life: helping people become better theologians. Although I am a theologian by trade, I am convinced that theology is for everyone—especially for
Christians.

What we believe shapes the way we live. And the way we live inevitably reveals our fundamental convictions about God, the world that he
has made, and our place in it. Even something as simple as bathing a child
or picking up a piece of trash can have profound theological implications.
So every Christian should strive to become a good, practical theologian—
someone who knows how to think clearly and biblically about everyday

life. As the apostle Paul said, ". . . we take captive every thought to make it obedient to Christ" (2 Cor. 10:5b).

I have been trying to help people become better theologians since at least 1995, when I first began serving at Philadelphia's Tenth Presbyterian Church under the late Dr. James Montgomery Boice. In those days my primary responsibility was to preach at the Sunday evening service. However, almost the first suggestion Dr. Boice made was that I should take a few minutes each week to analyze some current event or popular trend from the biblical point of view. Dr. Boice also knew what to call this new segment of the service: Window on the World. He borrowed this title from one of our predecessors, Dr. Donald Grey Barnhouse, who wrote a column called "Window on the World" for *Eternity* in the 1950s.

The Window on the World soon took on a life of its own. Each week I would address a different topic from the biblical point of view. That first year I spoke (among other things) about postmodernism, the decline of hell, eating (or not eating) at Christian restaurants, and Philadelphia's John Wanamaker, the famous Christian businessman who helped turn Christmas into a major shopping event. Soon church members started suggesting topics for me to address. They would leave magazine and newspaper articles in my mailbox at church, often with a note saying, "I thought this would make a good Window on the World."

The Window is still open almost every week, except during the summer, and it is regularly posted on the Tenth Presbyterian Church website (www.tenth.org). Over the years I have discussed everything from road rage to the Jesus Seminar, from the tulips in my window box to the portraiture of Vincent van Gogh. As of this writing, I have yet to run out of topics to address. In fact, ordinarily I have too many ideas to cover them all. There is always something happening in the world, and the Bible always has something to say about it. We are all theologians all the time!

By now you will have guessed that the essays in this book were first delivered as Windows on the World. As you can see from the table of contents, they cover a wide range of subjects—so many that it is hard to know how to introduce them. Perhaps the best way is to mention several important theological ideas that appear in many of the essays and that may help explain how to read them. These basic doctrinal concepts are multi-use items. That is to say, they can be used to help think through a wide range of cultural issues that confront ordinary Christians.

The first idea is that this really is "my Father's world." God made the world and everything in it. The God who has performed this marvelous work of creation is not an abstraction but a personal God who knows and cares what is happening in his world. He cares so much, in fact, that he has entered his world in the person of his Son and our Savior, Jesus Christ. And Jesus teaches us to address God the same way that he addressed him, calling him "our Father" (Matt. 6:9). The God who created the universe is our very own Father.

This means that whenever we open a window on the world, we gaze upon the person and purposes of our Father. God the Father is revealed in what he has made. As the Scripture says, "since the creation of the world God's invisible qualities—his eternal power and divine nature—have been clearly seen, being understood from what has been made" (Rom. 1:20). To know the world is to know the God who made it. This knowledge comes from what theologians call general revelation; that is, from what God has revealed about himself, in a *general way*, through his creation. Everyone, including non-Christians, can know true things about God from the world that he has made. The essays in this book explore the world with the ultimate purpose of knowing the God who created it as our Father.

General revelation is helpful as far as it goes, but it is incomplete without *special revelation*. This is the information God gives about himself through his written Word and also through his incarnate Word, Jesus Christ. What our Father has broadly revealed through his creation is more thoroughly explained in the Scriptures of the Old and New Testaments. The Bible is "God-breathed" (2 Tim. 3:16). Because it is the Word of God, it gives us our Father's perspective on the world that he has made and is working to redeem through Jesus Christ. The way to develop a completely

Christian worldview, therefore, is to study the Bible. Good theology is always biblical theology. With that in mind, every essay in this book draws explicitly on the teaching of Scripture.

Another important theological concept is four ideas in one. There are four basic conditions of humanity: creation, fall, grace, and glory. We were made perfect (creation), but sadly, through the sin of our first parents, we fell into sin (the fall). By his amazing mercy God has reached down to save us in Jesus Christ (grace) and ultimately to lift us up to his presence in heaven (glory).

I learned this simple and yet profound theological structure from Thomas Boston, a notable Scottish minister of the early eighteenth century, whose famous book on the subject was called *Human Nature in its Fourfold State*. Boston learned his theology from the scholars and pastors who wrote the Westminster Confession of Faith in the middle of the seventeenth century. They in turn learned it from various medieval theologians, who borrowed it from Augustine, the greatest theologian among the early church fathers.[1] But Augustine was summarizing the plain teaching of Scripture, where all these doctrines are found.

Creation, fall, grace, and glory—this four-part structure provides a basic theology for everyday life. These four principles tell us not only who we are but also who we were and who we will become. The doctrine of creation explains how God made things in the first place and what he made them for. The doctrine of the fall explains why everything has gone so badly wrong: it is all because of our sin. However, as we learn from the doctrines of grace, our Father has a plan for redeeming his world. This plan involves rescuing sinners from their fallen condition. Now by his grace, God offers forgiveness for sin and the free gift of eternal life through the death and resurrection of Jesus Christ. Although God's plan will not reach its fulfillment in this life, those who believe in Christ are destined to spend a glorious eternity with their Father in heaven.

This fourfold structure explains almost everything. It explains human relationships. We were created to have fellowship with one another, but we have been alienated and isolated by our fall into sin. Now by grace God is joining his people together to make one new humanity in Christ, a work that will come to its glorious completion with the communion of saints in heaven.

The same theological paradigm explains our work. We were created to serve God, but in our fallen condition the curse of sin turns our labor into toil. It is only by the grace of our Lord Jesus Christ that we are again enabled to serve God rather than men (Col. 3:23) as we wait for the glorious day when all our work will turn to praise.

To give yet another example, the same four ideas help to make sense of our physical environment. The universe was created for the glory of God. Yet the creation has been scarred by sin, and now it groans for its redemption from the fall (Rom. 8:20–22). Through his redeeming grace Christ is working to save the world—not just some of the people in it, but the world itself. This gracious work will reach its glorious conclusion in the new heavens and the new earth (2 Peter 3:13).

Variations on this four-part theme are scattered throughout *My Father's World*. All around us there are many happy reminders that our Father made this good world and everything good in it. At the same time, what is happening in the world provides many painful reminders of the way that sin distorts, disfigures, and destroys what God has made. All is not lost, however. Our Father is at work in his world and also in us. By his grace he is preparing us for glory. Thus some of the essays hint at the glory that is still waiting to be revealed. This is the right way to end, because the goal of all theology is the glory of God.

The essays that follow are much too short to offer anything like the definitive word on any of the subjects they address. They merely offer preliminary thoughts that invite further theological reflection. My prayer is that they will inspire you to become a better theologian by thinking clearly and biblically about our Father's world.

PART 1

CHRISTIANS IN THE WORLD

The world has a right to look upon us and make a judgment. We are told by Jesus that as we love one another the world will judge, not only whether we are His disciples, but whether the Father sent the Son. The final apologetic, along with the rational, logical defense and presentation, is what the world sees in the individual Christian and in our corporate relationships together.

—FRANCIS SCHAEFFER

*I*n the world, but not of the world—this is the Christian's constant struggle.

We are living in our Father's world. As his precious children we have a responsibility to serve him in every area of life and thought. We are called to use the powers of our minds, the affections of our hearts, and the strength of our wills to bring glory to God. We do not please him by withdrawing from the world. On the contrary, since the world is his creation, we find his pleasure by engaging with it in everything we think, say, and do.

But we do not belong to this world. That is to say, we do not participate in the sinful patterns of thinking and acting that have come to dominate it since the fall. As we live in the world our Father has made, we seek to avoid the contamination and corruption that have entered it by sin.

In one way or another, each of the following essays addresses our constant struggle to be in—but not of—the world. What enables us to survive this struggle and even to thrive as world-changing agents of divine transformation?

According to the Dutch art critic Hans Rookmaaker (1922–1977), only the grace of God can help us resolve

> the very practical problem of how we are to live in a world that is full of sin and ungodliness. Where things are loving, good, right and true, where things are according to God's law and His will for creation, there is no problem. The Christian will appreciate and actively enjoy and enter into all the good things God has made. But where they have been spoilt or warped by sin, then the Christian must show by his life, his words, his action, his creativity what God really intended them to be. He has been made new in Christ, been given a new quality of life which is in harmony with God's original intention for man. He has been given the power of God Himself by the Holy Spirit, who will help him to work out his new life into the world around him.[1]

Yes, God is working through us by his Spirit, who is not from this world but is able to bring new spiritual life into it.

1

INWARD CHRISTIAN SOLDIERS

$\mathscr{S}$ometime in the late 1990s, *The New York Times Magazine* ran a story about a Christian family from Allentown, Pennsylvania. The lead for the article read, "Abandoning the fight for a Christian America, fundamentalists are retreating into their own homes." The story described how one family of nine lives the Christian life within the walls of their white farmhouse.

The family's stated goal is "not to participate in those parts of the culture that do not bring glory to God." To that end, they do not go to the mall. They do not watch television. They do not listen to popular music. They do not go on dates, although when the children grow older they will be allowed to pursue courtship under parental supervision. They do not play sports because, says the mother, the team environment breeds "behavior that we would not deem Christlike." The children do not even go to Sunday school, so as to avoid the evils of age segregation in the local church.

The New York Times Magazine interviewed the family from Allentown because they represent a significant change in Christian attitudes about American culture. There was a time when American culture *was* Christian, when the biblical worldview shaped the public agenda. Obviously that is no longer the case. We are living in increasingly post-Christian times.

Since the 1970s, many evangelical Christians have tried to regain cultural territory by pursuing political power. In many ways, that strategy has failed, with the result that evangelicals are now starting to give up on political solutions to cultural problems. This analysis is confirmed by an editorial in *Christianity Today*,[1] written by the political strategist Paul Weyrich. Although Weyrich was at the forefront of Christian political engagement during the 1980s, he now advocates what he calls "a strategy of separation" in which Christians "bypass the institutions that are controlled by the enemy." "We need to drop out of this culture," says Weyrich, "and find places, even if it is where we physically are right now, where we can live godly, righteous and sober lives." The family from Allentown has followed Weyrich's advice. They are separating from, dropping out of, and bypassing American culture.

It is good for Christians to recognize the limits of politics. We are called to be good citizens, but we must never look to the government for salvation. We are called to build the kingdom of God, not establish a Christian America. But to what extent are we called to separate ourselves from American society? Does Christ call us to be *onward* Christian soldiers or *inward* Christian soldiers?

This is a question Christians have always faced. How can we be in the world without being of the world? Jesus prayed about this when he went to his Father to intercede for the church. Jesus said to the Father, "[My disciples] are not of the world, even as I am not of it" (John 17:16). Yet he also said, "My prayer is not that you take them out of the world but that you protect them from the evil one. . . . As you sent me into the world, I have sent them into the world" (John 17:15, 18). In other words, our Lord has prayed that we would reach the world without becoming worldly.

It is not easy to know where to draw the line between being in the world and of the world. Some separation is required. There are places it is not wise for Christians to go. There are things it is not good for us to see or to hear. As a result, we often find ourselves out of step with American culture. The piece in *The New York Times Magazine* noted, with some amazement, that Christianity is now a countercultural movement. In the 1960s, the counterculture questioned authority. Now everyone questions authority . . . except Christians, and that makes us countercultural.

It is one thing to stand against sin, but it is another thing to drop out of American culture, which God has not called us to do. There are ways in which the family from Allentown is not so much countercultural as it is anticultural. I am reminded of medieval times, when the church retreated to its cloisters and its monasteries. The remnants of Christianity were preserved, but Europe was abandoned to its sins.

It is not my place to decide where Christians should shop or which television programs they should watch. These are matters of freedom, which each Christian has the responsibility before God to determine. It is my place, however, to issue a reminder that while Christ calls us to separate ourselves from sin, he does not call us to separate ourselves from sinners. I worry that Christians are retreating from American culture at a time when people desperately need the gospel. Christ does not call us inward but onward and outward, to reach our friends and our families with bold, persuasive, thoughtful, and compassionate Christianity.

We should not remove ourselves from places where we have opportunities to stand for Christ against the sins of our culture. Christians are called to coach Little League, but not to yell at the ump; to work for the corporation, but not to disparage the management; to exhibit work in the art show, but not to give in to despair; and so on. When we engage in these kinds of activities, we always run some risk of becoming worldly. Nevertheless we do them because we are called to be in the world to the glory of God.

2

THE ACCIDENTAL EVANGELIST

*M*ore than half the human beings who have ever existed are alive in the world today. This statistic has a number of significant implications. One is that there are more people on this side of eternity than there are on the far side. Or to put it another way, during the twenty-first century the combined population of heaven and hell will double.[1]

With the eternal destiny of more than half the human race hanging in the balance, this is no time to be an Accidental Evangelist. By an Accidental Evangelist I mean a Christian who has no real intention of ever leading anyone to Christ. An Accidental Evangelist is a genuine Christian who trusts in Jesus Christ for salvation, reads the Bible, and goes to church. But there is one thing Accidental Evangelists do not do, and that is to make a deliberate effort to share their faith. If they ever do lead anyone to Christ, it happens more or less by accident.

I invite you to become an Intentional Evangelist, to make it your particular goal to help lead people to a saving knowledge of Jesus Christ. We are commanded to "go and make disciples of all nations, baptizing them in the name of the Father and of the Son and of the Holy Spirit, and teaching them to obey everything [Jesus has] commanded" (Matt. 28:19–20a). But we will never fulfill that Great Commission until we adopt the attitude of the apostle Paul, who became "all things to all men so that by all possible means" he "might save some" (1 Cor. 9:22b).

The most important thing an Intentional Evangelist does is to live in constant communion with Christ, depending daily on his grace. There is something attractive about a person who lives in such intimate fellowship with God that others are drawn to know God for themselves. The trouble is that so few of us have entered very deeply into the soul of authentic Christianity. Robert Coleman, who is one of the world's leading experts on evangelism, recently observed that "the problem of evangelism is that we're trying to work out of a context where the people themselves are not living in the fullness of the Spirit. . . . I'm talking about being filled with the Holy Spirit. I'm talking about being in the very presence of the living Christ so that his love is flowing through you and you are fulfilling the Great Commandment, and in that love you are making disciples."[2]

Once you begin to live in communion with Christ, the next thing is to pray for people to come to a saving knowledge of Jesus Christ and to pray for them by name. Make a list of unsaved neighbors, co-workers, family members, and friends, and ask God to make them his dear children. This is what my colleagues and I do in an evangelistic prayer meeting every Friday during lunchtime. We take the names that people give us and pray for their salvation. We continue to be amazed at God's faithfulness in answering our prayers. In the past years we have seen dozens and dozens, maybe even hundreds, of people become Christians.

As Intentional Evangelists pray for the lost, they also place themselves at God's disposal. It is dishonest to ask God to save someone unless we are willing to be part of the conversion process. So ask God to give you opportunities to share your faith. My prayer is that God will allow me to help one person become a Christian. As soon as that person makes a commitment to Christ, I start praying for someone else to help. But the main thing is to place ourselves at God's disposal.

Once we have offered ourselves to God as Intentional Evangelists, we will find that there are countless ways to share our faith. One is to mention our church activities to friends. Once they know that we are Christians, everything we do will represent the love of Christ. But until they know that Christ is first in our hearts, they can only guess why we live and love the way we do. Learn how to introduce Christian perspectives into everyday conversations. Learn how to be bold without becoming obnoxious. Say things like, "Well, as a Christian, I . . . "

Another way to share our faith is to invite a friend to church. The Bible teaches that salvation comes from hearing the preaching of God's Word (Rom. 10:14–17). This means that inviting people to church is still the best way to bring them to Christ. Consider inviting a business colleague to a Bible study or bringing a friend to a special worship service.

Pass out copies of Christian literature. I sometimes receive letters from people who have read one of my books. I am most pleased when these letters come from people who received a copy from a Christian friend.

Participate in ministry. Whether feeding the homeless, tutoring internationals, or learning to speak in American Sign Language, there are many ways to teach the Bible and call people to faith in Christ.

Be creative! Start a Bible club for neighborhood children. Study the Bible with a Jewish friend and share how Christ fulfills the promises of the Old Testament. Throw a dinner party that includes Christian and non-Christian friends. Host a four- or five-week study to investigate Christianity. Start a book club and use literature as a vehicle to discuss spiritual issues. Once we become Intentional Evangelists, God will show us how to use our gifts and interests to do his work.

While eating breakfast in a city diner, I watched the great masses of humanity on their way to work—more than three hundred thousand of them in all. It occurred to me that they are all on some sort of pilgrimage, heading for eternity. Where will they end up? If we want to help some of them find their way to heaven, we will want to become something more than Accidental Evangelists.

3

LIVING IN
APOSTOLIC TIMES

*W*hen King David assembled his great army to defeat King Saul he was joined by two hundred sons of Issachar, "with all their relatives under their command." The Scripture says that the sons of Issachar were men "who understood the times and knew what Israel should do" (1 Chron. 12:32). Surely these men were among David's most trusted advisors! Nothing is more valuable to a king than counselors who understand the times and know what to do.

What would the sons of Issachar say to us? How should we understand our times, and what should we do about them?

It is often said that we are entering a new era. The rising generation—

Generation X—does not accept the authority or answers of its elders. Christianity is on the decline, crowded out by an upsurge in paganism. The world is shrinking as the Internet enables instant communication to span the globe. On top of everything else, we have entered a new millennium.

But our era is not so new after all. Many of the obstacles and opportunities we face in the world today are the same obstacles and opportunities faced by the New Testament church. We are really living in apostolic times.

Our culture is similar to the culture of the early church in at least four ways. First, the apostolic times were religious times. The New Testament is careful to explain how Christianity differs from mystery religions, idol worship, Greek philosophy, Judaism, and paganism. This is because, from the beginning, the good news about Jesus Christ had to compete for an audience. The apostles preached the gospel in the context of religious pluralism.

Our times are just as religious. Think of the rise of Islam and Scientology in America. Think of the interest people take in horoscopes and psychic hotlines. Think of all the false preachers on television. Or think of the way that weight loss, television, psychotherapy, sports, singles bars, militia movements, and feminism have become religions unto themselves.

One of the reasons Christianity had to compete with so many religions was that the world was shrinking. So a second similarity is that the apostolic times were international times. International trade and travel exposed people to the latest ideas from other cultures. First Greek and then Latin became international languages. The apostle Paul was able to keep up a lively correspondence with churches all over the known world.

Our times are just as international. Every day we have access to news from all over the world. Electronic mail is shrinking the globe once again. The export of music, food, and clothing from the United States is making American culture the dominant culture of the world. The world looks to New York the way it once looked to Rome.

Third, the apostolic times were immoral times. Consider the city of Corinth, one of the great cites of Asia Minor and a leading cultural center. The apostle Paul once listed some of the common sins of Corinth: sexual immorality, idolatry, adultery, prostitution, homosexual acts, theft, greed, drunkenness, and slander (1 Cor. 6:9–10). Then, as he ran his finger down the church rolls, he realized that many members of the Corinthian church had been enslaved by these very sins. "And that is what some of you were," he wrote (1 Cor. 6:11). Early Christians worshiped in the center of sin city.

The same is true today. Adultery is ripping the American family apart at the seams. We worship dozens of idols. Some neighborhoods are well known for homosexual sin. We live in a nation that seems to be founded on greed. When people talk about the American dream, they are usually craving a bigger piece of the pie. Or what about slander? Consider the nasty way our politicians speak about one another, or the juicy headlines in the tabloids, or the insults family members trade on television.

Finally, the apostolic times were dangerous times. The powers of this world tried to stamp out the church almost before it started. The missionary journeys of Paul were dangerous not only for him; they were dangerous also for the churches he visited. According to tradition, most of the apostles became martyrs.

Our times are just as dangerous, if not more so. More Christians have been martyred for their faith in the twentieth century than in all previous centuries combined. We can thank God that the sword has not yet been turned against Christians in the United States, but we still suffer with Christians in other lands. We know that our brothers and sisters in places like South America, China, and the Middle East are being intimidated and even killed for their faith.

We are living in apostolic times. We live in a global village marked by religious pluralism and moral indifference. It is a difficult, even a dangerous time to be a Christian.

If we are living in apostolic times, then what should we do? The answer is obvious: we should live like the apostolic church. We should live the way the people of God lived during the days of the New Testament. The apostle Paul told them to "live peaceful and quiet lives in all godliness and holiness" (1 Tim. 2:2). We should aspire to live the same way, asking God to make us sons and daughters of Issachar, who understand the times and know what to do.

4

BECOMING AN
APOSTOLIC CHRISTIAN

How should we understand our times, and what should we do about them? In the previous chapter, I tried to show that we are living in apostolic times. We face many of the same obstacles and opportunities faced by the New Testament church. The apostolic times were religious, international, immoral, and dangerous times.

What should Christians do when they live in apostolic times? First, because we live in religious times, we must be biblical Christians. At the end of Acts 2 we read that the first Christians "devoted themselves to the apostles' teaching" (Acts 2:42). If that sounds familiar, it is because we still do the same thing. Week after week, we go to hear the Scriptures of the Old and New Testaments explained and applied. Day after day, we study the Word of God so that we can hear and obey God's voice.

A biblical Christian—a Christian who is devoted to the apostles' teaching—is not distracted by other religions. We live in an age of religious pluralism. Some modern theologians say that the mere existence of other religions denies the uniqueness of Christianity. They say that the more we know about the religions of the world the more difficult it is to believe that Jesus Christ is the only way to God. This is nonsense. The claim that Jesus Christ is the only way of salvation was never made in ignorance. The writers of the New Testament were well aware that other religions offered other kinds of salvation. The apostolic times were religious times, and it was because they lived in religious times that the apostles insisted that there is only one true Savior: Jesus Christ.

Second, because we live in international times we must be world Christians. A world Christian has a passion for missions. A world Christian is concerned about the work of the church throughout the whole world.

The apostolic Christians were world Christians. The Book of Acts is the story of their quest to take the gospel into the entire world. This is such an urgent quest that Paul's arrival in the great city of Rome comes as the climax of the book: "For two whole years Paul stayed [in Rome] in his own rented house and welcomed all who came to see him. Boldly and without hindrance he preached the kingdom of God and taught about the Lord Jesus Christ" (Acts 28:30–31). The apostles had a heavy burden to share the gospel with the whole world, and they did not rest until that burden was lifted.

We carry the same burden. One of the catchphrases of Generation X is "think global, act local," but that is not a choice world Christians care to make. We think and act biblically, and that means thinking and acting locally *and* globally. Every time we share the love of Christ with international students, every time we put money in the offering plate for missions, every time we go on a short-term mission trip, we are sharing in the worldwide work of the gospel of Jesus Christ. We are acting as world Christians.

Third, because we live in immoral times we must be holy Christians. That is what the apostle Paul told the first Christians to become when they were living in immoral times. He told them to live "peaceful and quiet lives in all godliness and holiness" (1 Tim. 2:2b). Christians are supposed to be different. We do not swear. We do not cheat on our taxes or our spouses. We do not worship money or sex. We do not resign ourselves to racism; we are committed to reconciliation. We *do* love our neighbors. We care for the poor. We defend widows, orphans, and the unborn. We welcome strangers. We cherish our families. The more immoral our times become, the more holy our lives ought to become.

This is especially true when times are dangerous. Because we live in dangerous times, we must be bold Christians. As I've pointed out, the 20th century was the most dangerous Christians have ever faced. But intimidation and persecution do not hinder the work of the church. In fact, danger tends to make Christians even bolder than they would otherwise be. This is why Tertullian (c. 160–c.220) said, "The blood of the martyrs is the seed of the church." There was something a little bit reckless about the apostles, as if they enjoyed nothing more than being shipwrecked, imprisoned, or roughed up by an angry mob, as long as they had a chance to share the good news about Jesus Christ. Dangerous times demand bold evangelism.

Are you a son or a daughter of Issachar? Do you understand the times? Do you know what to do? When you hear the voices of many religions, be a biblical Christian, holding fast to salvation in Christ alone. When you hear news of trouble in the world, be a world Christian, praying for the worldwide progress of the gospel. When you are tempted to sin, be a holy Christian, resisting temptation for the sake of Christ. And when you are frightened, be a bold Christian, living dangerously in your witness for Christ. We are living in apostolic times, and apostolic times call for apostolic Christianity.

5

ALIEN RESIDENCE

The things I learn about my wife continue to amaze me, even after more than a decade of marriage. Recently I have discovered that the love of my life is an alien. Admittedly, from time to time I have entertained the notion that our kids might be aliens. And now I know why . . . they get it from their mother!

Perhaps I should explain. After ten years of moving from apartment to apartment Lisa and I suddenly bought a house in the big city. We have become homeowners, as people say.

The strange thing is that we do not think of ourselves as owning anything. On the contrary, we have a strong sense that our house belongs to the Lord and that we are merely looking after it for him.

This seems to be the attitude every Christian should take about every home. The Bible teaches that this world is not our permanent residence. Our life on earth is only temporary. In the words of the old hymn, "This world is not my home, I'm just a-passing through." The apostle Peter went so far as to describe Christians as "aliens and strangers in the world" (1 Peter 2:11), which is why I say I am married to an alien. (And so, I hasten to admit, is my wife.)

Every Christian is a resident alien. For the time being we live on earth, so we are residents. But our real and eternal home is in heaven, so we are aliens. As the apostle Paul explained to his friends in Philippi, "our citizenship is in heaven. And we eagerly await a Savior from there, the Lord Jesus Christ" (Phil. 3:20). The Philippians knew what Paul was talking about because some of them enjoyed the privilege of Roman citizenship. Although they lived in Philippi, they looked to Rome for their safety and their identity. In the same way, Christians think of themselves as citizens of heaven, even while they live on earth.

If Christians are resident aliens, then the house Lisa and I bought is an alien residence, a house invaded by aliens. Although we live, eat, work, play, and sleep there, our eternal home is somewhere else.

Thinking of one's home as an alien residence is a great help when things go wrong. When somebody spills a brownie on the carpet, or when the furnace starts making strange clunking noises, or when the basement gets flooded, it is wonderful to remember that we aren't going to live here forever anyway. As Scripture says, "The time is short. From now on . . . those who buy something [should live] as if it were not theirs to keep; those who use the things of the world, as if not engrossed in them. For this world in its present form is passing away" (1 Cor. 7:29–31).

Everything in this world will soon disappear. Even what we own will not belong to us forever, including the house we bought. Our present accommodations are temporary. There are no homeowners in this world, only tenants; no buyers, only renters.

In order to help us remember that we live in short-term housing, Lisa and I invited ninety of our closest friends to help dedicate our house to the Lord. I began the brief service by reminiscing about my Dutch ancestors.

They came to America in the nineteenth century seeking religious freedom. When they arrived in Pella, Iowa, they adopted a Latin motto that
can still be read on the front of the town's first church: *In Deo Spes et
Refugium*, or "In God is our hope and refuge."

Our family has turned that civic motto into a domestic one. We hope
our home will be a safe haven for friends, relatives, neighbors, parishioners,
missionaries, internationals, and needy people in the city. But our house is
not our refuge. God is. As citizens of heaven we have made our eternal
dwelling place with him. So wherever we live and wherever we go, God remains our only refuge.

The house dedication included the reading of Scripture, prayer for the
safety and ministry of the house, a doxology, and a household benediction
(2 Sam. 7:29). One of the Bible passages we read was appropriate for the
city, which is where Lisa and I have chosen to raise our family. The passage
came from a letter the prophet Jeremiah once sent to Jews living in the
wicked city of Babylon.

The Jews would have given anything to leave Babylon behind, with all its
paganism and corruption. But God told them to do the opposite. He said, "Build
houses and settle down; plant gardens and eat what they produce. . . . Also, seek
the peace and prosperity of the city to which I have carried you into exile. Pray
to the LORD for it, because if it prospers, you too will prosper" (Jer. 29:5, 7). In
other words, "invest everything you have into the common life of the city. Live
there, work there, pray there. Then you and your city will prosper."

My wife finds it humorous that Jeremiah's letter was written to exiles.
There are times when she feels as if I have carried *her* into exile. She longs
for the wide-open spaces and the purple mountain majesties of her Colorado childhood. But we have made a commitment to one another and to
the Lord to seek the welfare of the city, even to buy a house there. For the
sake of the kingdom of God we are called to be civic-minded Christians.

But we will not be exiles forever. Someday Lisa will get back to her
beloved mountains, if not in this life then in the life to come. After all, our
house here is only an alien residence. Some day we will go home.

6

THE WANAMAKER
NAME

C hristmas in Philadelphia will never be quite the same. Children used
to go downtown to Wanamaker's to see the Wanamaker's Light
Show. Now they go to Lord and Taylor to see the Lord and Taylor Light
Show, but the Wanamaker name has vanished.

In Philadelphia around the turn of the twentieth century, it would have
been different, because in those days it was almost impossible to avoid the
Wanamaker name.

Shortly before Christmas in 1850, a twelve-year-old boy named John
Wanamaker (1838–1922) entered a jewelry store to buy a gift for his
mother. Just as the storekeeper was wrapping the gift, he saw something

36

else he liked better. "It's too late," the storekeeper said, "you've already bought this." It was then that the young John Wanamaker made his vow: "Some day I'll own a store, and I'll treat my customers kindly and fairly."[1]

And so he did. John Wanamaker was a gifted merchant. He established four cardinal principles of business that became the "platform of modern business":

- Return of money if buyer returns goods, uninjured, in ten days
- A guarantee to each buyer stating terms of sale
- No second price
- Any article may be exchanged, if desired, within two weeks of purchase

Although it was opened during the difficult years of the Civil War, Wanamaker's annual sales surpassed two million dollars by the end of its first decade. (That was when two million dollars was a lot of money!) Seventy thousand customers came to Wanamaker's when the new store was first opened, a sign that in time the store that offered "Everything from Everywhere to Everybody" would become the largest retail store in America. It was the first to send buyers to foreign markets, to have electric lights, to have air conditioning, to use newspaper advertisements, to have a profit-sharing plan for employees, to offer two weeks' free summer vacation, and, believe it or not, to offer daily weather forecasts to the public.

Much of the store's commercial success came from the integrity of its business practices. This advertisement was typical of Wanamaker's honesty: "Men's ties. They're not as good as they look. But they're good enough. 25 cents." The store couldn't buy enough "good enough" ties to keep up with the demand!

John Wanamaker was also a churchman. When President Benjamin Harrison appointed him Postmaster General of the United States, Wanamaker traveled a total of more than one hundred thousand miles to be present at worship every Sunday. In all, he founded and built four different

Presbyterian churches. For sixty years he was the superintendent of the Sunday school he established. By 1900 the Bethany Mission School, as it was called, had an average attendance of more than five thousand young people every Sunday, four thousand of whom Wanamaker knew by name.

John Wanamaker was an evangelist. This is what he had to say about helping someone to "receive the Savior," as he usually called conversion:

> If you once have the joy and sweet pleasure of bringing one soul to Christ, you will be hungry to get to another. Do not argue, do not be rebuffed, be patient and gentle and keep on with a prayer in your heart and drop a good word here and there as you go along. Oh, what a pleasure it will be to you to have a newborn soul beside you at the next Supper of the Lord.

Wanamaker organized, hosted, and paid for the Dwight L. Moody (1837–1899) evangelistic meetings in Philadelphia in 1875. To do so, he delayed the opening of his new store, saying, "The new store can wait for a few months for its opening; the Lord's business comes first." More than a million people attended the Moody meetings.

Wanamaker also established the Bethany Brotherhood, a group of nearly a thousand men who promised to "pray daily for the spread of Christ's kingdom among men" and to "make an earnest effort to bring at least one man or one boy within the hearing of the Gospel of Jesus Christ." The epitaph given to Wanamaker at Bethany Collegiate Presbyterian Church is a suitable one: "By reason of him many went away and believed on Jesus."

John Wanamaker was a missionary statesman. At age twenty, he began to provide leadership to the fledgling Philadelphia YMCA in the days when it really was the Young Men's Christian Association. He was first introduced to the Philadelphia YMCA as "the young man with the funny name that no one has ever heard of." They became familiar with his name soon enough. Wanamaker organized hundreds of open-air summer evangelistic meetings held all over Philadelphia. Over the years, he also provided the money to build YMCA facilities in Madras, Calcutta, Seoul, Kyoto, Peking, and Russia.

John Wanamaker was also a peacemaker. His contacts with African-American clergy in Philadelphia led to the foundation of the "Colored Branch" of the YMCA. Wanamaker served on the first Interracial Committee of the organization and provided the funds for them to purchase their own building.

John Wanamaker was a patriot. During his brief tenure as Postmaster General, he initiated the parcel post, rural free delivery, and commemorative postage stamps. He also trained some fourteen hundred of his employees for military service in World War I.

John Wanamaker was a patron of the arts. He brought the famed Wanamaker organ to Philadelphia in 1911. He also displayed massive paintings of Christ before Pilate and Christ on Calvary in his store during Easter. (The paintings have since been sold.)

John Wanamaker was a man of personal godliness. His testimony was that he "gave his heart and life to God at fifteen." As far as anyone is able to tell, he walked with God ever after. When the financial markets faltered in 1907 and it was rumored that his business was about to fail, he wrote in his diary, "I am just going on day after day with a heart strong in the belief that the Heavenly Father has me in his keeping and will guide me to do for me what is best." This is how he prayed for his Sunday school students:

> We will make heart-room for Jesus, Thy Son, the name to sinners most dear. We live in the grace of His redeeming love and our only hope is the finished salvation of Calvary.
>
> Empty-handed, full of sin; sad of heart and conscious of aggravated wickedness, we cast ourselves at thy feet, O Christ. God be merciful to me a sinner.

John Wanamaker even had something helpful to say about Christmas: "Christmas is a Man born, not a sentiment."

The details of the life of John Wanamaker suggest three practical observations. First, we could use a few men and women of the caliber of John Wanamaker. In a time of declining godliness, we could use more men and women who are vigorous in their work, generous with their money, loyal to the church, affectionate toward children, and zealous for the gospel.

Second, names do not last very long on this earth. None of us is likely to attain anything like the cultural influence or civic renown of John Wanamaker. Among his pallbearers were the senators and governor of Pennsylvania, the mayors of New York and Philadelphia, Chief Justice William Taft, William Jennings Bryan, and Thomas Alva Edison. The public schools were closed on the day of his funeral. Nevertheless, just seventy-five years later, the Wanamaker name has all but disappeared. Almost the only place you can still see it is on his statue on the east side of Philadelphia's City Hall (unless Lord and Taylor has taken that as well!). We may be assured that our own names, too, will one day vanish from this earth.

Third, the Lord remembers the names of the righteous. Even when the names of godly men and women have disappeared from all earthly remembrance, they are carefully and perfectly marked by the living God in his Book of Life. The promise of Psalm 112:5–6 was true for John Wanamaker, as it is for every believer: "Good will come to him who is generous and lends freely . . . a righteous man will be remembered forever."

7

More Than a
Restaurant

*S*omeone gave me a news clipping with an advertisement for a culinary establishment called The Inner Circle. Underneath the restaurant logo the ad read:

> The first all Christian restaurant—New Jersey's newest spot for elegant dining, fun & fellowship—Come and experience the finest international dishes from Cajun, pasta, Jamaican, Chinese & soulfood.

The Inner Circle boasted a full schedule of activities. Thursday featured "Fellowship Happy Hour" from four to six, followed by "Business

Networking Night." Friday night was "Singles Mingle" night with a live Christian jazz band. The joint really started hopping on Sunday morning with "Breakfast Sunday School" (kids eat free), followed by "Brunch in the Spiritual Realm." The slogan at the top of the ad said it all: "It's more than a restaurant . . . It's a ministry."

My question is whether The Inner Circle is more than a restaurant or less than a ministry. One place to answer that question is in John 17, the passage where Jesus prayed to his heavenly Father on behalf of his church. Dr. James Montgomery Boice once pointed out that the things Jesus did *not* pray for were almost as important as the things he did pray for. Jesus said, "My prayer is not that you take them out of the world. . . . They are not of the world, even as I am not of it. . . . As you sent me into the world, I have sent them into the world" (John 17:15–18).

The problem with places like The Inner Circle is that they do the opposite of what Jesus prayed that we would do. They take Christians out of the world. Evangelicals are always doing this sort of thing. We withdraw into our own institutions, hosting our own radio programs, starting our own cable networks, publishing our own books, and advancing our own political lobbies. We have our own music festivals and entertainment awards. Now we even have our own restaurant!

At the same time, we do all of those things in a worldly way. For example, when we set up an all-Christian restaurant, we have things like Fellowship Happy Hour and Business Networking Night. This is the opposite of the way the Lord wants us to do things; We are not in the world any more, but we are of the world. Instead of being a counterculture, we have become a subculture.

The wisdom of Jesus' prayer to send Christians out into the world was pressed home for me one Saturday night at a restaurant. After a theology conference, some of us went out to eat, and as we were eating, the chef sat down to join us (and also to promote his new cookbook). Our church administrator entered into a discussion with him, and after they had chatted for a while, the chef asked what we were all doing at the restaurant. The administrator explained that we had been at a conference on Reformed theology, at which point the chef asked the obvious question: "What is Reformed theology?"

People who ask that kind of question need to be careful who's listening, because they might get more answer than they bargained for. In this case, the church administrator was sitting on one side of the chef, and I was sitting on the other. At the time I had just completed seven years of advanced education, learning all about Reformed theology. Up to that point I hadn't really been part of the conversation, although I had briefly prayed that the Holy Spirit would guide it. It's not every day that somebody asks what Reformed theology is. When it happens, it's nice to have your pastor handy. My church administrator was only too happy to say, "Phil, maybe you'd like to answer that question." The three of us proceeded to talk about spiritual things for the next hour or so.

When people ask what Reformed theology is, the place to start is with the gospel. I didn't use any Latin terminology, but I quoted plenty of Scripture, talking about theology based on the authority of Scripture alone, about salvation by the righteousness of Christ alone, and about justification by grace alone, through faith alone, all to the glory of God alone.

It was the kind of conversation that is bound to occur when we are out in the world. As we bump into people, our Christian faith has a way of spilling over into our conversations with them.

I don't know what will happen in the life of the chef. He was a devout Roman Catholic, given to intense fasting and prayer. We sensed that he was still on a spiritual quest and that he desired a deeper communion with Christ than he had yet experienced. It may be that he was not far from the kingdom, and I pray for his salvation.

What I do know is this: that conversation was one small part of the answer to the prayer that Jesus prayed—and the prayer that he didn't pray—for the church. Jesus Christ prayed two thousand years ago that his people would be sent out into the world to complete his work, not that they would be taken out of the world. Our little conversation was included in that prayer. And when that prayer was answered in the course of our sharing the gospel, the restaurant was more than a restaurant. It was a ministry.

PART 2

THE BIBLE

The Bible is the source of authority for our creed, the substance of what we are to believe, and it is the handbook of our conduct, the directory of all our duties and obligations to the Lord, to our own souls and souls of others. . . . We believe the Bible to be inspired of God, absolutely, and therefore inerrant, infallible, authoritative, with a dominant, a predominant influence upon our thinking and our manner of life.

—MARCUS BROWNSON

The Bible is God's Word. God has given us this Word in the form of stories, poems, histories, letters, and prophecies. Together these writings tell us everything we need to know about our Father and his world. They explain why he created the world and why our sin has made things go so badly wrong. They also tell the story of salvation. They announce the good news of God's grace: the forgiveness of sins and the hope of eternal life through the death and resurrection of Jesus Christ.

The Bible's unique authority makes it an obvious place for God's enemies to attack. The supernatural origin and divine perfection of Scripture are constantly under assault. During the last half of the twentieth century the conflict raged around biblical inerrancy—the doctrine that the Bible is free from error as it was originally written. Evangelicals called this conflict "the battle for the Bible."

That particular battle has ended, but the warfare is not over. The historical accuracy of the Bible remains a significant topic of contemporary interest. At Christmas and Easter the major news magazines can still be counted on to run cover stories somehow related to the Bible. Often these articles address some allegedly new theory about the Bible's original historical context. And when it comes to new theories about the Bible, the stranger the better, at least as far as the media are concerned. The reason is obvious: the Bible sells. People are still fascinated by its teaching, especially when there seems to be some controversy surrounding it.

All of this makes it necessary for Christians to continue to defend the accuracy and authority of the Bible. Ultimately, accepting the Bible as God's Word depends on the inward testimony of the Holy Spirit, speaking through Scripture. It is a matter of faith, which comes only as a gift from God.

This faith is not unreasonable, however. On the contrary, there are many good reasons to believe that the Bible is credible, even down to the smallest detail. Some of these reasons are explored in the following essays, which in one way or another were prompted by recent attacks on scriptural authority. Of all the reasons to defend the Bible against such attacks, the most important is this: its historical accuracy helps to confirm its saving message.

8

DEAD SEA SCROLLS
AT FIFTY

*I*n 1947 a young shepherd named Muhammad el-Dhib set out to find one of his goats. The animal was lost somewhere in the foothills beside the Dead Sea. As the boy searched, he threw stones at the caves high up the cliffs. He watched one stone disappear into the mouth of a cave, and then he heard an unexpected clink, the sound of pottery breaking.

When Muhammad scrambled into the cave to investigate, he discovered large clay jars with scrolls inside. It turned out to be the most important archaeological find of the twentieth century and the greatest manuscript discovery of modern times. When all the dust had settled, archaeologists unearthed parts of some 870 scrolls concealed in eleven different caves. They have been known ever since as the Dead Sea Scrolls.[1]

The Dead Sea Scrolls were written one hundred years and more before the birth of Jesus Christ. In those days a small, devout religious community lived in the wilderness at Qumran, not far from Jerusalem. Probably they were known as the Essenes. Certainly they were devoted to studying the Bible. The scholars at Qumran carefully copied entire books of the Hebrew Bible and hid them in caves for protection. The Dead Sea Scrolls include 220 biblical scrolls, representing every book of the Old Testament except Esther.

Over the past fifty years the Dead Sea Scrolls have shed new light on the Essenes, on the text of the Bible, and on Judaism in the days of Jesus. Yet complete information has been hard to come by. A secretive group of Jewish and Catholic scholars have kept many of the manuscripts to themselves. In some cases they have hoarded scrolls for decades, waiting until they can publish commentaries before releasing their texts for the perusal of other scholars.[2]

By 1991 an evangelical scholar named Martin Abegg had waited long enough. He used secret channels to obtain a copy of a concordance that had been completed in the 1950s. Once Abegg had the concordance, he painstakingly entered it into a computer and reproduced the text of the Dead Sea Scrolls.

Now that all the Dead Sea Scrolls finally have been released to the public, we can state confidently that they confirm the reliability of Holy Scripture. The conclusion reached by the editor of the first Qumran scrolls remains valid: "The essential truth and the will of God revealed in the Bible . . . have been preserved . . . through all the vicissitudes in the transmission of the text."[3] Or, to quote the Puritans, "The Old Testament in Hebrew and the New Testament in Greek, being immediately inspired by God, and, by His singular care and providence, kept pure in all ages, are therefore authentical."[4]

Most modern translations of the Hebrew Bible are based primarily on the Masoretic Text, which dates from around A.D. 1000. The Masoretic Text is a copy of a copy of a copy (and so on) of the original autographs of the Old Testament. The Dead Sea Scrolls were written by 100 B.C. In other words, the Dead Sea Scrolls were written more than a millennium before the Masoretic Text on which our English Bible is based.

How do these two editions of the Old Testament compare? Do the Dead Sea Scrolls agree with the Masoretic Text? Or has the Bible been corrupted over the centuries?

It turns out that the Masoretic Text and the Dead Sea Scrolls are virtually identical. Consider the magnificent Isaiah scroll, one long scroll containing all sixty-six chapters of the book of Isaiah. The Isaiah scroll from Qumran and the best English translations agree 99 percent of the time! That figure is now accepted as the general degree of similarity between the Dead Sea Scrolls and the Masoretic Text.

What about the remaining 1 percent? This is where Bible scholars earn their keep. The task of determining which manuscripts are the most accurate has begun. In some cases, the Dead Sea Scrolls shed new light on problem passages.

Take Goliath, for instance. Skeptics have long scoffed at the idea that the giant Philistine was 9 feet, 9 inches tall. That figure may be anatomically possible, but it does stretch the imagination. Interestingly, the Samuel scroll found in one of the caves at Qumran gives his vital statistics as 6 feet, 9 inches tall, which was gigantic nonetheless, but less improbable.

Or consider something Stephen said in his sermon at Pentecost: "Joseph sent for his father Jacob and his whole family, seventy-five in all" (Acts 7:14). For those who believe in the inerrancy of the Bible in its original autographs, as I do, this verse has always posed a problem. The Masoretic Text says Jacob's family numbered seventy, not seventy-five (Gen. 46:27). So which is it? The Dead Sea Scrolls say seventy-five, which means that Stephen may well have been quoting from the Hebrew original.

Another disputed verse is Psalm 22:16:

Dogs have surrounded me;
    a band of evil men has encircled me,
      they have pierced my hands and my feet.

This is a crucial verse for Christians because it describes the sufferings of the Messiah, Jesus Christ. The reference to pierced hands and feet is obviously a prophecy about the crucifixion. Yet the Masoretic Text renders it differently: "Like a lion are my hands and feet." Happily, a recent book by Peter Flint proves from the Dead Sea Scrolls that "pierced" is the preferred reading.[5]

Some puzzles from the Dead Sea Scrolls still need to be solved, like a shorter version of Jeremiah, or versions of the psalms that contain 89, 150, and 151 chapters, respectively. But the Dead Sea Scrolls mainly serve to confirm the reliability of the Holy Bible.

It is a wonderful thing to know that we can trust our Bible. It is also wonderful to know that we can trust the Savior who is introduced in its pages. His name is Jesus, and he was the one who said, "I tell you the truth, until heaven and earth disappear, not the smallest letter, not the least stroke of a pen, will by any means disappear from the Law until everything is accomplished" (Matt. 5:18).

9

TREASURES IN
THE SAND

*G*oliath's Skull Found Near Jerusalem," the headline read. I couldn't resist reading the rest of the article. On March 23, 1993, Dr. Richard
Martin discovered a skull in the valley of Elah, in the foothills of Judea,
where David's battle with Goliath took place. The skull was enormous.
"But," Dr. Martin explained, "the most telling piece of evidence is the small
round rock we found embedded in the forehead. . . . There was also evidence to suggest that the head had been severed from the body by a sharp
object, most likely a sword."[1]

Subsequent tests revealed that the skull was roughly three thousand
years old. Anyone who gets A's in math knows that the skull dated to

about 1000 B.C. And anyone who gets A's in history knows that 1000 B.C. matches exactly to the time period of King David.

I haven't heard anything more about this discovery since, so I don't know what other scholars have concluded about Dr. Martin's find. Some of them, I am sure, think the whole thing is a bunch of nonsense. And they might be right. A tomb discovered in Israel in the mid-1990s was said to contain the graves of the Maccabees, but that has since proven to be a misunderstanding. Biblical scholars always need some time to argue about their findings before they reach certainty. And in this case, there would be no way to prove for certain that the skull did belong to Goliath.

But the discovery of this skull—Goliath or no Goliath—is not the only recent discovery of interest to the church. In 1979, for example, an Israeli archaeologist found two tiny scrolls in a tomb in Jerusalem, dating from 600 B.C. When they were unrolled, the scrolls turned out to be inscribed with the earliest extant biblical text: "The LORD bless you and keep you; the LORD make his face shine upon you and be gracious to you; the LORD turn his face toward you and give you peace" (Num. 6:24–26). This was the priestly blessing that the Lord gave to Moses.

In 1986 archaeologists deciphered some clay document markers they had purchased from Arab dealers in 1975. What they discovered is that one of the markers bears the seal of Baruch, son of Neriah. Baruch was the scribe who copied down the words of the prophet Jeremiah (see Jer. 36). Another marker bears the seal of Jerahmeel, the son of Jehoiakim who was sent on an unsuccessful mission to arrest Jeremiah and Baruch (Jer. 36:26). Baruch and Jerahmeel were thus proven to be historical figures. Since those earlier discoveries a second seal has been discovered from the hand of Baruch, this one with a thumbprint on the edge. For the first time, we not only have material evidence for the existence of biblical characters, but we have their very fingerprints.

In 1990, an Egyptologist at the Field Museum in Chicago used hieroglyphic clues to identify figures on a wall at Luxor as the ancient Israelites. The hieroglyphics, which come from 1200 B.C., celebrate an Egyptian victory over Israel, providing extrabiblical proof of Israel's existence as a nation more than three thousand years ago.

Three years later, scholars digging at Tel Dan found an inscription from 900 B.C. that included the words "House of David" and "King of Israel." Until that discovery, some scholars actually doubted that King David existed. Later the French scholar André Lemaire also identified the phrase "House of David" on the Moabite Stone in the Louvre.[2]

More discoveries are on the way. There are more than three hundred active digs in Israel. Recently a bowl dating from A.D. 100 was discovered in a fishing village on the shores of Galilee. It was decorated with a cross, which came as a big surprise to scholars who maintained that the cross did not become a Christian symbol until the third or fourth century!

New excavations have begun in four new caves at Qumran, where the Dead Sea Scrolls were discovered. The possibility of the recovery of more biblical manuscripts is tantalizing. A report is also expected on new evidence for the proper location of the ark of the covenant on the temple mount.

Christians should welcome these digs and pay attention to whatever treasures are pulled from the sand. Archaeology reminds us, again and again, that the Bible is a book of history, and reliable history at that. This is why evangelical Christians have never been afraid of biblical archaeology. If the Bible were historically suspect, archaeology would be a threat and an embarrassment to the evangelical church. But most of the best archaeologists, especially in the early days of the discipline, carried a toothbrush in one hand, so they could brush away the dust of antiquity, and a Bible in the other, so they would know where to brush.

It's true, of course, that archaeological evidence is sometimes used to discredit the Bible. Not long ago, some members of the Society of Biblical Literature denied the existence of Moses, the giving of the law at Mount Sinai, and the parting of the Red Sea. Their argument was that we don't have any material evidence for Moses, so we don't know for sure that he existed. Their position is that unless something can be proven to be historical, it's not historical.

There are a number of problems with this kind of argument. To begin with, these scholars usually don't allow the Bible to be used as historical evidence. That's poor scholarship, because the documents that make up the Bible are historical documents. For most matters, the Bible is all the historical evidence we need.

Another problem with this kind of archaeology is that it depends on an argument from silence. Such an argument is based on what we don't hear, not from what we do hear. It's an argument from what we don't find, not from what we do find, an argument from what isn't there, rather than what is. What some archaeologists will say about a man like Moses is that we don't have any positive evidence that proves his existence, so he probably didn't exist. We can't hear him or see him, so he must not be a real historical figure. It's not that they have any evidence that actually disproves that Moses existed; it's just that we don't have any evidence to prove that he did.

Some arguments from silence are sound arguments. If I go home at the end of the afternoon and my home is quiet, that's a strong argument that no one is home. If I shout "Anybody home?" and I don't get an answer, then I am certain. But I wouldn't be quite as certain if I lived in a much bigger place, like Buckingham Palace. If I walked through the royal entrance and heard nothing but silence, I couldn't make a strong argument that no one was home. Even if I shouted "Anybody home?" I still wouldn't be sure that there weren't any royals in one of the apartments. The only thing I could say is that I didn't know for sure whether or not anyone was home.

In the field of biblical archaeology, arguments from silence are usually weak arguments. It's true that apart from the Bible, we don't have any positive evidence for the existence of Moses, but that's hardly surprising. Given the size of the area he traveled, given the way things deteriorate (even in the Middle East), and given the way that sand covers everything up, it is no surprise that we haven't found any extrabiblical evidence for Moses, or for most other biblical figures. At least we haven't found any yet. Arguments from silence work only until someone hears something. It used to be that we didn't have any evidence for Baruch or Jerahmeel, either. But now we do.

In the meantime, absence of evidence is not evidence of absence. In other words, the absence of extrabiblical evidence for Moses isn't evidence that he was absent from history. So the testimony of the Bible should be allowed to stand on its own merits. The noteworthy thing is that no archaeological discovery has yet disproven the facts of the Bible. From the standpoint of biblical history, everything we have found in the sand has been treasure.

16

THE STEALTH BIBLE

*I*n 1997 a major controversy erupted within evangelical publishing. Under the headline "The Stealth Bible,"[1] *World* magazine announced that Zondervan planned to introduce a gender-neutral edition of the New International Version (NIV) of the Bible. To understand what that meant, it helps to know that Zondervan is a major Christian publishing house, that the NIV is the translation found in the majority of evangelical pews, and that a gender-neutral translation is one that avoids masculine references whenever possible.

The decision to publish a neutered Bible met with a storm of protest. Many Christian leaders were alarmed that the decision to go gender-neutral was made by a publisher rather than by the church. They were also concerned about the confusion that would result if two versions of the NIV were available simultaneously.

Under duress, Zondervan abandoned its plans to make gender-related changes to the NIV. They had already begun to sell an inclusive-language NIV in England but agreed to pull it off the shelves. For months afterward, the gender-neutral NIV sold like wildfire on the evangelical black market.[2] Then in 2002 Zondervan reversed directions and announced that it was going forward with its original plan to sell a new translation called *Today's New International Version* (TNIV).

One alarming aspect of the controversy over the TNIV is that decisions about the Word of God are now made primarily on the basis of economics. Bible publishing is big business, especially when a publisher can tap a new market. However, one good result of the original flap was a series of "Guidelines for Translation of Gender-Related Language in Scripture." The purpose of these guidelines was to ensure that the Bible more evangelicals use than any other (NIV) remained accurate. Unfortunately, the publication of the TNIV means that Zondervan no longer supports the guidelines it formerly accepted.

In some cases, accurate translation means using gender-neutral language. Here are some examples. In Matthew 12:36 Jesus says, "I tell you that men will have to give account on the day of judgment for every careless word they have spoken." The word for "men" in that verse is the Greek *anthropoi*, which refers to people in general. So the verse accurately can be translated, "On the day of judgment, people will have to give an account for every careless word they speak."

Another example comes from Matthew 16:24, where the King James Version reads, "If any man would come after me." But in Greek the verse does not say "man." It uses the indefinite pronoun *tis*, which means "anyone." So the NIV has it right: "If anyone would come after me."

On many other occasions, however, gender-neutral language leads to incorrect translations. The most obvious example would be using feminine pronouns to refer to the Godhead. God does not have a gender, but Jesus taught us to call him Father. Thankfully, the revision of the NIV does not even consider referring to God as "our Mother in heaven."

Similarly, God the Son should be called "man." The TNIV strays from this usage. For example, instead of saying, "It is better for you that one man die for the people," Caiaphas the high priest says, "It is better for you that one *person* die for the people" (John 11:50). Jesus Christ is a person, but he also has a masculine gender. Therefore it is proper to refer to him as a man.

This is especially true when the Bible draws a comparison between Adam and Jesus. It was as a man that Adam represented his fallen race, and it was as a man that Christ redeemed his people: "For if, by the trespass of the one man, death reigned through that one man, how much more will those who receive God's abundant provision of grace and of the gift of righteousness reign in life through the one man, Jesus Christ" (Rom. 5:17).

This raises the question of whether or not the term "man" ought to be used to refer to the human race in general. What was once standard English is now frowned upon in academic circles, where referring to "mankind" arouses a storm of protest. Yet this is the way God first addressed humanity: "When God created man, he made him in the likeness of God. He created them male and female and blessed them" (Gen. 5:1b–2a). Here we see the true equality of men and women. The man and the woman were made in the image of God.

Yet God proceeds to use the term "man" to refer to male and female alike: "And when they were created, he called them 'man.'" (Gen. 5:2b; see also Gen. 1:26–27). Therefore using the term "man" to refer to human beings in general is not a relic from patriarchal times. It is not a human invention; it comes from the mouth of God.

One more translation issue is particularly difficult to resolve. How should the word "son" (Greek *huios*) be translated? "You are no longer a slave, but a son; and since you are a son, God has made you also an heir" (Gal. 4:7). It is difficult for God's daughters to think of themselves as sons. So perhaps it would be better to say, "You are no longer a slave, but a child." The problem is that this obscures an important fact of law in the ancient world. The full rights of inheritance belonged only to sons. Thus the point is that every child of God receives a full inheritance in Christ.

Incidentally, men have the same difficulty when the church is described as the bride of Christ (e.g., Eph. 5:25–27; Rev. 21:2). It will not do to say that the church is the "spouse" of Christ. The Bible definitely intends to say that Christians are a bride for Christ: pure, virginal, and beautiful.

When it comes to brides—or to sons—biblical images must be understood the way God means them. The Word of God has to be taken by faith, trusting God includes trusting him to say what he means and mean what he says. To translate the Bible inaccurately is to misquote God and to mistrust him. And whenever God is misquoted or mistrusted, he is misrepresented and misunderstood.

Most Bible believing Christians will probably decide to avoid using *Today's New International Version*. Instead, they may prefer to use the new translation that most literally and accurately follows the best guidelines for translation, including the translation of gender-related terminology: the *English Standard Version*.

THE JESUS SEMINAR

*T*he Jesus Seminar began when a group of thirty scholars decided "to renew the quest of the historical Jesus and to report the results of its research to more than a handful of biblical scholars." Whether they have discovered the historical Jesus or not is debatable, but they certainly have communicated their findings to more than a handful of Bible scholars. The results of the Jesus Seminar have been widely reported in American newspapers, on National Public Radio, and even on *Larry King Live*.

The fruits of their labors are also available in *The Five Gospels: The Search for the Authentic Words of Jesus.*[1] For those wondering about that arithmetic, the Jesus Seminar includes the unreliable Gospel of Thomas (which omits the death and resurrection of Jesus) among the five gospels of Jesus Christ.

Probably the best thing that can be said about the *Five Gospels* of the Jesus Seminar is that it's a colorful book. The texts of the Gospels are printed in four colors, reflecting four degrees of certainty about the reliability of the biblical text. At seminar meetings, scholars were given colored beads to use as they voted on each text. Red represented words definitely spoken by Jesus; pink was for words probably spoken by Jesus; gray was for words probably not spoken by Jesus; and black was for words definitely not spoken by Jesus. The book's introduction explains the code as follows:

> Red: That's Jesus!
> Pink: Sure sounds like Jesus.
> Gray: Well, maybe.
> Black: There's been some mistake.

Indeed, there has been some mistake. The methodology and results of the Jesus Seminar are riddled with so many problems that it is hard to know where to begin to critique them. Their work is laughable, from a scholarly standpoint. They deserve our scorn. After all, they've earned it.

To begin with, the Jesus Seminar does not represent a consensus of reputable scholarship. Promotional material for the Jesus Seminar asserts that "the scholarship represented by the Fellows of the Jesus Seminar is the kind that has come to prevail in all the great universities of the world." Hardly. Most of the participants have earned their doctorates, but they are not, as they claim to be, "independent, neutral observers." What the Jesus Seminar amounts to is a club of idiosyncratic academics on the lunatic fringe of biblical criticism. Especially when it comes to the Bible, Christians do not need to be intimidated by appeals to scholarly consensus. One always needs to know "Which scholars?" and "From where?" and "Why?"

In this case, the question of why is especially pertinent. One of the primary purposes of the Jesus Seminar is to write a new gospel. Robert W. Funk, the seminar's leading figure, explained the intentions of his fellow scholars like this: "What we need is a new fiction . . . a new narrative of Jesus, a new gospel, if you will, that places Jesus differently in the grand scheme, the epic story." In Funk's view, what has been holding us back from having a new gospel is the evangelical church. He claims that "the religious establishment has not allowed the intelligence of high scholarship to pass through pastors and priests to a hungry laity." Another member of the seminar likes to say that Christians who trust their Bibles are "intellectually frozen at age 12." This leads me to wonder if some Christian middle schoolers should challenge some of these scholars to a battle of wits!

How does the Jesus Seminar decide which sayings of Jesus belong in their new gospel? One of the basic principles of their work is the "criterion of dissimilarity," which says: The only things that we can prove Jesus said are things that don't sound like either the Jewish tradition or the Christian tradition. And if what Jesus says sounds like the Old Testament, then it probably wasn't his idea in the first place. If what he says sounds like the Christian church, then later Christians were probably putting their ideas into the mouth of Jesus when they wrote the Gospels. That's a little bit like some historian saying that the only things we can be sure John F. Kennedy said are things that no other Democrat ever said!

The problem with the criterion of dissimilarity is that if we take the Judaism out of Jesus and the Christianity out of Christ, we aren't left with very much gospel. Almost everything in the Gospels turns out to be either too Jewish or too Christian to be Jesus! That's why more than 80 percent of *The Five Gospels* is printed in black ink, the color for things that Jesus definitely did not say.

It hardly seems necessary to warn Christians about the Jesus Seminar. A Christian ought to be able to smell scholarship this foul a mile off. However, some Christians may want to be warned that a movie is in the works. Paul Verhoeven, the director of such unedifying movies as *Basic Instinct* and *Showgirls*, attended the Jesus Seminar with a view to making a Jesus film. Here is how he described his plans: "To be honest, I don't have an agenda. I'm just doing what's important to me." But of course, doing what's important to oneself *is* an agenda. It's the kind of self-serving agenda that drives secular Bible scholarship like the Jesus Seminar. To do what is important to oneself is often to fail to do what is important to God.

When it comes to the Gospels, God has an altogether different agenda. It's the same agenda he announced when Jesus was transfigured on a high mountain: "This is my Son, whom I love; with him I am well pleased. Listen to him!" (Matt. 17:5b). To put it another way, if we're voting on the authenticity of Jesus' words in the Gospels, all we need are red beads.

LOVE, MARRIAGE, AND FAMILY

There is no society more near, more entire, more needful, more kindly,
more delightful, more comfortable, more constant, more continual,
than the society of man and wife, the main root, source,
and original of all other societies.

—Thomas Gataker

The family is breaking apart. This is widely known. By any observable measure—the divorce rate, reported cases of domestic violence, the number of children growing up without a father, just to name a few—more families are failing than at any previous time in American history. One searches in vain for a trend pointing to a positive future for the family.

What is perhaps less widely recognized is that singleness is also under attack. Perhaps this is a necessary corollary to the collapse of the family. When families fail, singles will fail too. Whatever the reason, many singles are struggling to find their place in the world. They move from one job, one relationship, one apartment, and one church to the next. This rootlessness often leads to discontent, insecurity, and even despair.

The lack of community and cohesion among singles and couples is a sign that American society is in serious disarray. What can be done?

The greatest resource for marriage or singleness is not some self-help manual or psychological technique but the Bible. And whatever our situation in life, the best place to find the kind of friendship and fellowship that will help us flourish is (or at least ought to be) the church.

The basic principles for family life are all found in the Bible: the family is a covenant community; wives are to love their husbands with the kind of submission that God the Son offered God the Father; husbands are to love their wives with the kind of sacrifice Christ made for the church; children are to obey their parents; parents are to nurture their children. The basic principles of singleness are also found in the Bible: chastity, contentment, self-sacrifice, and single-hearted devotion to God.

Many of these principles stand in direct opposition to the ideals of popular culture. In fact, rearing a godly family and answering Christ's call to singleness have become radical, almost subversive acts. In order to persevere in our respective callings as single and married men and women, we need the help of God's counterculture: the church. Our Father's house provides the caring community where singleness and marriage can flourish for the glory of God.

The essays that follow address a variety of contemporary problems inside and outside the family. They offer basic biblical principles for romance, love, marriage, and family, including old age. They also touch on several areas of family life that are not directly addressed in Scripture. This is where wisdom comes in—the kind of godly, practical wisdom that can be found only in the church.

12

THE NEW HARLEQUIN
ROMANCE

*T*here is a new trend in the publication of Harlequin romance novels. I've never read a book from Harlequin—or any other romance novel, for that matter—but I have seen the covers at the newsstand. Lots of covers: Harlequin sells 150,000,000 books a year.

A recent article from the Institute for American Values notes that a number of recent Harlequin romances focus on the theme of fatherhood.[1] The books have titles like *Do You Take This Child?*, *The Secret Baby*, *The Father of Her Child*, and so forth. The basic plot line goes something like this: A man and a woman meet. They are attracted to one another sexually. She gets pregnant. Then, for one reason or another, they separate.

Maybe he's not ready to make a commitment, or circumstances conspire to keep them apart, or she's afraid to tell him that she's pregnant. The situation gets desperate. She is facing a life of loneliness, and her baby is facing a life without a father. But at the very last moment, he confesses his undying love for both her and the baby, they get married, and they all live happily ever after.

To get the flavor of the new Harlequin romance, consider Dr. Sheila Pollack, the heroine of *Do You Take This Child?* Dr. Pollack is about to become an unwed mother. The baby in her womb was conceived during a night of passion with Slade Garrett, who has long since disappeared. On her way to the hospital she laments having to rear a child without a father. But then, to her amazement, Slade shows up at the maternity ward, proposing marriage. He has decided that he wants to be a husband and a father after all. He wants, he says, to take the time "to stop and smell the baby powder."

The good news about the new Harlequin romances is that couples are getting married and fathers are taking responsibility for their children. What is strange about them is the sequence of events, which changes all the old rules for courtship. The traditional chronology was love, marriage, sex, and baby. It was like the old schoolyard rhyme: "First comes love, then comes marriage, then comes baby in a baby carriage."

The new chronology is a plot for postmodern times: sex, baby, marriage, and love. It is almost exactly backwards, except that the baby still comes after the sex. But this is simple biology, and not even Harlequin can change the way God made us. Otherwise, the new romances turn romantic relationships upside down, making sex the basis for love and separating procreation from marriage.

The Bible is not a handbook on courtship and marriage, but it does put things in the right order. First comes love, a selfless commitment to care for another person. Then comes marriage, a covenant partnership made in the sight of God (see Mal. 2:14), in which both partners promise undying love. This is followed almost immediately by sex, the uniting act that cements their covenant. Last of all comes the baby, depending on the will and providence of God.

This order of events goes all the way back to Genesis: "A man will leave his father and mother and be united to his wife [that's marriage], and they will become one flesh [through sexual intercourse]" (Gen. 2:24). Not only is this the biblical pattern, it is the only sequence that makes good sense. Arranged marriages sometimes work, but ordinarily a man and a woman should start loving one another before they promise to stay in love for the rest of their lives. And they should get married before they start enjoying sexual intimacy. There are lots of good reasons for this, but one of the most obvious is that children need the security of being born into a family that is based on a covenant commitment.

This biblical sequence—love, marriage, sex, baby—has many practical implications. For married people, it serves as a reminder that love is the foundation of the marriage. There are many ways to strengthen a marriage: renewing wedding vows, giving one's spouse sexual pleasure, and sharing the joys and trials of parenting, to name a few. But perhaps the best way to strengthen a marriage is to go back to the foundation, which is loving one's spouse. For a wife, this means serving her husband (Eph. 5:22–24), helping him become the man God wants him to become. For a husband, this means sacrificing for his wife (Eph. 5:25–28), cherishing her in a way that nurtures her inward beauty. God's best plan for marriage requires husbands and wives to become good lovers (Prov. 5:15–20).

The biblical pattern also has practical implications for single people. One is that Christians who are unmarried should refrain from explicitly sexual intimacy. True sexual fulfillment is to be found only within a marital covenant, never outside of it. Sex was never designed to provide the foundation for a relationship, let alone a marriage.

This is where the new Harlequin books do readers their greatest disservice. The new romances suggest that the way to get a man to make a commitment is to carry his child. This is not romance; it is fantasy! Women sometimes hope that they can trade sex for commitment, but that is almost never the way life works, especially when a baby is involved. True love waits. Single men and women should protect their purity and their virtue by preserving their sexuality for marriage.

The biblical pattern for courtship and marriage also shows singles where to begin. The first step is love, which is the greatest commandment. Love is something we can offer right away. The more we love—through service and sacrifice—the greater our capacity for intimacy. If we ever get married, we will discover that we already know how to be good lovers. If not, we find that our growing ability to love is widening our network of satisfying friendships.

Love, marriage, sex, baby. We depart from this sequence at our peril, although God always has grace for sinners. Whether we are married or single, following God's pattern brings the deepest joys and the most lasting pleasures.

13

ADAM HAS TWO DADDIES

*A*dam Gallucio[1] has two daddies. Or, to be more accurate, Adam has one parent he calls "Daddy" and one he calls "Father." The state of New Jersey agreed to allow Jon Holden and Michael Gallucio to adopt two-year-old Adam. This decision made New Jersey the first state to allow gay and lesbian couples the privilege of joint adoption.

Holden and Gallucio had already been serving as Adam's foster parents. When they first tried to adopt the boy, their request was denied. New Jersey previously had refused to allow any unmarried couples, whether homosexual or heterosexual, to adopt children who were wards of the state.

After the two men initiated legal proceedings against the state, New

Jersey changed its policy. When asked why they didn't adopt Adam individually, as other gay couples have done, the proud new parents said, "This is a family. . . . That would be unacceptable."

What is a family? Gay parenthood creates unprecedented social and ethical dilemmas. What does a preschool teacher say when a gay couple asks her to endorse their application for adoption? Should you attend the worship service if your lesbian sister invites you to her son's baptism? These are the kinds of questions Christians increasingly face.

The New Jersey policy says something about the changing status of homosexual couples in contemporary society. The gay and lesbian agenda is to get Americans to treat homosexuality as normal, and marriage is one of the last bastions of normalcy in America. The Gallucios are trying to give homosexuality greater credibility. What could be more normal than two men getting married and starting a family? A lawyer from the Lambda Legal Defense and Education Fund hailed the New Jersey decision as "a statewide recognition that lesbians and gay men make fit and loving parents and that gay couples should be treated equally with straight couples."

To their credit, Holden and Gallucio seem to have been motivated by compassion. When Adam came to them as a three-month-old foster child, he was suffering from liver, lung, and heart damage because his biological mother was a drug addict. They undertook this adoption because they believed it to be in the best interests of the child.

Whether having two daddies is in Adam's long-term interests is debatable. There is the question of stability. The reason New Jersey has refused to grant adoptions to unmarried couples in the past is because families without vows tend to fall apart. Then there are the confusing questions Adam will undoubtedly face about his identity, sexually and otherwise.

But I am less interested in what the Gallucio adoption says about homosexuality than in what it says about marriage. We live at a time when marriage is being redefined. Many people refuse to live within its bonds. Others define it to meet their designs. "Marriage is a personal lifestyle choice," they say. "It is any two people who love each other." They are afraid of making the mistake of a lifetime, so they write their own marriage vows, promising to be devoted to one another "as long as we both shall love."

That is not how God defines marriage. He ought to have the right to define it because he invented it. God is the one who saw that it was not good for man to be alone. God is the one who made a suitable helper and brought her to the man. God is the one who said, "For this reason a man will leave his father and mother and be united to his wife, and the two will become one flesh" (Gen. 2:24). God is the one who defined marriage as one man and one woman united in a love covenant for life.

To define marriage any other way is to abuse it. In testimony given before the Maryland state legislature in March 1997, Robert Knight said,

> Giving same-sex relationships or out-of-wedlock heterosexual couples the same special status and benefits as the marital bond would not be the expansion of a right, but the destruction of a principle. One can no more expand the definition of *marriage* than one can expand the definition of a yardstick and still use it as a reliable measure.[2]

America is fast becoming a nation where people can make a yardstick any length they like. When asked if it would be difficult for Adam to be reared by gay men, his new father responded that since only 30 percent of children are now being reared in a home with a father and a mother, "he's going to be in the majority."

If that statistic is accurate, then this is an important time to be a Christian. The more confused our society gets about marriage, the more vital Christian marriages will become. Instead of going with the flow, we have a chance to be countercultural. Eventually, uniting as one man and one woman to rear a covenant family may become the most radical of all lifestyles. If people want to know what a marriage is supposed to look like and how a family is supposed to operate, the only place they will be able to go is to the church.

This is a reminder to honor the institution of marriage. Those who are not married should encourage those who are. Singles should also keep themselves sexually pure so as not to undermine their own or anyone else's future marriage.

Those who are married must maintain the vows they have made before God and the church. This means renewing our commitment to love our spouses. It means keeping our promise to stay married until death. We need to remember that marriage means one man and one woman united in a love covenant for life, in case everyone else in the world forgets.

14

NO SURRENDER

*L*aura Doyle has written a popular book called *The Surrendered Wife: A Practical Guide to Finding Intimacy, Passion, and Peace with a Man.*[1] I picked up a copy at a local bookstore, and you should have seen the look on the clerk's face when she realized what I was buying!

The author wrote *The Surrendered Wife* because she believes something is wrong with the average American marriage. In particular, she believes that wives ought to give up their struggle to gain power and control over their husbands. In a word, they ought to surrender.

Doyle reached this conclusion by way of experience. She realized that much of the conflict in her marriage was caused by her desire to control her husband. Their relationship did not improve until she gave up that battle. "Stop trying to control everything," she learned to say to herself. "Surrender."

Some of the book's practical suggestions for surrendering have been controversial. Put down the checkbook, wives are told, and leave it there. If you need money for daily expenses, ask your husband to give it to you . . . in cash. And when you're in the car, let your husband find his way, even if he doesn't know how to get there. It's more important for him to be in charge than to know where he is.

But the book's main point is that women should stop trying to be in control: "A surrendered wife . . . relinquishes inappropriate control of her husband, respects her husband's thinking, receives his gifts graciously, expresses what she wants without trying to control him, relies on him to handle household finances, and focuses on her own self-care and fulfillment." As a result, she is "vulnerable where she used to be a nag, trusting where she used to be controlling, respectful where she used to be demeaning, grateful where she used to be dissatisfied, and has faith where she once had doubt."[2]

In some ways *The Surrendered Wife* sounds like the biblical pattern for marriage. Respect your husband. Don't be critical. Don't nag. If you say something rude, apologize. When he does something nice for you, say, "Thank you." This is common-sense advice for any relationship. It is all part of what the Bible means when it tells us to be kind to one another.

The book is also right to recognize that men and women are different. As Doyle puts it, there should be "one skirt and one pair of pants." And of course this is part of God's intention for marriage, that husbands and wives should complement one another. After decades of efforts to claim that women are exactly the same as men, the pendulum now seems to be swinging back in the other direction. *Vive la différence!*

The problem is that husbands and wives both want to be in charge. Here the book's analysis is essentially correct, or at least half correct. When a partnership becomes a power struggle, it cannot thrive. We read all about this in Genesis 3:16, where God announces the marriage penalty of sin: the woman desires to master the man, while the man seeks to dominate the woman. *The Surrendered Wife* does not talk about sin, in so many words, but it is basically right to encourage wives to give up control. (Obviously this is easier to do when husbands set aside their desire to dominate and love their wives with caring sacrifice.)

What is strange, however, is the motivation for surrender, which ultimately is selfish. The point of the book is that surrendering is the best way to guarantee personal happiness. It is something a woman does—not to obey God or to love her husband, but—to get what she wants out of life. In fact, it turns out that surrendering is not a way of giving up power but a way of gaining it. When a woman stops trying to control what her husband does, she gains more control over her life. Surrendering is just a more sophisticated and more effective way of getting what she wants.

God's design for marriage does not require surrender but submission. The Bible says, "Wives, submit to your husbands as to the Lord" (Eph. 5:22). It is important to be clear what the difference is. In fact, one of the reasons the biblical ideal of submission is so unpopular in our day is that women think that submission *does* mean surrender. They assume that to submit is to be subservient and therefore to give up one's identity.

To surrender is "to give oneself up into the power of another." To submit, by contrast, is to "yield to authority." Submission is not about power and control, but about authority. In the case of marriage, it is about the spiritual authority that God has given to husbands in the home.

Submitting to authority does not mean that wives shouldn't let their husbands know when he is out of line. There are many appropriate ways to let someone in authority know when he is making a mistake, and one of the ways that wives love their husbands is by showing them the error of their ways. Perhaps the best biblical example of this is Sarah, who is commended for her submission to Abraham (1 Peter 3:5–6), but who also let him know when he was acting against God's will for their family. In fact, God told Abraham to listen to his wife (Gen. 21:12). To submit is not to surrender but to be a joyful, creative, intelligent, loving partner. Wives who submit in this way have God's blessing, for they are conformed to the image of Jesus Christ, who submitted to the will of his Father (see Matt. 26:42; 1 Cor. 11:3).

15

FATHER AND SON

*S*ince becoming a father, I have learned a good deal about fatherhood and even more about sonship. When I look at my son Joshua, it is like seeing myself in one of those mirrors that makes objects appear smaller than they are. I see myself, only on a smaller scale. And I hear myself too. Some of our dialogues sound familiar, as if I have heard them somewhere before. Let me give a few examples.

One spring we went to the Azalea Garden at the Philadelphia Museum of Art, and we found a little playground on the other side of Kelly Drive. When we got there, Josh, who was almost four at the time, managed to climb up to a place from which he could not climb back down, and he spent the rest of our time being too scared to let me help him get back down to the ground. When he finally gave in and trusted me enough to let me lift him down, I said, "There. Now, was that so bad?" Josh told me that, yes, in his opinion, it was so bad.

Here is another example. I wanted to take Josh to the mall north of the Liberty Bell to play hide-and-seek in all the archways. Josh had other plans. He couldn't remember ever going to that mall before, and he couldn't quite see the point. So I said something like this:

> Look, I want to take you to a new park to play some new games together. It's going to be great; it's going to be even better than the Stage Coach Park, but you're going to have to trust me. I know you've never been there before, but I've been there, and trust me, it's going to be great.

Eventually we did go the mall, and it *was* great. We played hide-and-go-seek, tennis-ball tag, soccer, and basketball. On our way home we had a conversation that went something like this:

> "Thanks for going to the mall with me, Josh. We had the best time, didn't we?"
>
> "Ya."
>
> "Now, before we went, did you trust me that we were going to have a good time?"
>
> "Ya."
>
> "No, you didn't! You didn't even want to go, but I was right, wasn't I? You have to learn to trust me."

God the Son said much the same thing to Simon Peter after he took his little excursion on the Sea of Galilee: "You of little faith, why did you doubt?" (Matt. 14:31).

There is another little conversation Josh and I have had dozens of times. My big speech in it goes like this: "Have I ever let you down before? No, seriously, Josh, have I ever dropped you before? In your whole life, have

I ever dropped you, even once?" God has a speech like that too: "I will never leave you nor forsake you" (Josh. 1:5b).

My other regular speech is even shorter: "Stop whining." That is what the Lord God said to the children of Israel when they were grumbling in the wilderness (Ex. 16:1–12), and what he said to the Philippians: "Do everything without complaining or arguing" (Phil. 2:14).

We keep having conversations in which Josh sounds like me talking back to God, and I sound almost like I am quoting God from Scripture. What I am learning from these conversations is that the basic problem with sons is that they want to be dads. Often they do not believe that their fathers know what they are doing, and so they want to be the dads of their lives. (Daughters have the same basic problem.)

We came in from playing outside one evening, and Josh didn't think he was ready to go to bed yet, so he said, "It's my choice. I can do whatever I want to do." I was reminded of Jeremiah 6:16, in which God says,

> "Stand at the crossroads and look;
>   ask for the ancient paths,
>   ask where the good way is, and walk in it,
>   and you will find rest for your souls.
>   But you said, 'We will not walk in it.' "

Sons tend to be skeptical, argumentative, and headstrong. They are better at complaining than they are at trusting. In short, they are an awful lot like their dads. Their dads have trouble being good sons to their heavenly Father for all the same reasons.

The only difference is that sometimes dads can see things from a father's point of view. This means that we get a taste of what it is like for God the Father when his sons and daughters grumble, argue, and wander. It is heartbreaking.

What fathers want from their sons is trusting love. Every once in a while, I feel as if I am actually getting through to Josh. "I trust you, Daddy," he said not long ago. "I know you won't let me down. I can trust you because you love me. You're the best daddy in the whole world!"

That is what fathers always love to hear from their sons and daughters, and our Father in heaven is no exception.

16

FATHERLESS AMERICA

*S*omehow Father's Day doesn't seem quite as important as Mother's Day, but I doubt whether there has ever been a more important time to be a father.

Some sociologists have identified a generation they are calling the Millennials, or the Bridgers. These are children born between 1976 and 1996, and they represent one-fourth of America's population. Generally speaking, the Builders were the generation that won World War II; the Boomers were the last generation to have stay-at-home moms; the Busters are the Generation Xers in search of an identity; and the Bridgers are the bridge to the new millennium.[1] For at least the next half century, they will be the most influential people in the world.

Many dads have Bridgers living in their homes. But not all dads, because many Bridgers do not live with their fathers. At any given time, nearly one-third of all children eighteen and under do not live in the same home with their fathers, and less than half spend their entire childhood with both of their parents.[2] Our country is fast becoming a fatherless America.

Tragically, when we look at the problems Bridgers are going to face, almost all of them turn out to be problems that dads are supposed to solve. Experts say that Bridgers face a future of economic uncertainty; they lack moral boundaries; they live in a culture of rising violence; and they are unclear about their gender roles. Those are exactly the kinds of things that fathers are for. Fathers are supposed to provide for the material needs of their families. They are supposed to teach the difference between right and wrong and to show what it means to be gentle as well as strong. Fathers, more than anyone else, teach their sons what it means to be men *and* their daughters what it means to be women.

Many of the problems Bridgers face stem from being fatherless. That is also true of their most serious problem: a crisis of faith. Bridgers are being reared in a world without absolutes. Although they have some interest in spiritual things, they have little or no interest in organized religion. One young man spoke for many when he said, "You know, to me God means the 'main guy.' And the 'main guy' means different things to different people. I got friends who find God in ways that are totally different from me. But ultimately it's the same—it's God."[3]

Bridgers have been inoculated against the idea that one religion is any better than any other. In fact, they have been trained to be suspicious of anyone who claims to know the truth. "I get real angry," said one Bridger, "at these Christians who tell me that Jesus is the only way to heaven. I mean, what kind of arrogance is that?"[4]

Given these attitudes, it comes as little surprise to learn that while 60 percent of their grandparents, 40 percent of their parents, and even 25 percent of their older siblings claim to be Christians, only 4 percent of the Millennial generation will profess faith in Jesus Christ.[5]

What can dads do about this? To put the question another way, What can a father do to promote the spiritual welfare of his home?

The first thing a father can do is improve his own spiritual welfare. Generally speaking, the best way to strengthen a family's faith is to strengthen the faith of its father. Whatever spiritual changes need to take place in a household must begin in a father's heart. Christian fathers constantly need to rededicate themselves and their families to the glory of God.

Another thing a father can do is cherish his wife. All the love in a household flows through the love a father has for the woman he married. More than anything else, what gives children confidence to face the world is the absolute certainty that their dad will always care for their mom. A father's love for his wife may even be more important to his children than his love for them. Children learn what love is from their father's heart. This is part of what the prophet Malachi meant when he promised that God would "turn the hearts of the fathers to their children" (Mal. 4:6).

What else can a father can do to shore up the foundation of his household? He needs to provide for his family, of course. The importance of this is sometimes overlooked, but providing for his family is a father's God-given responsibility (see 1 Tim. 5:8). However, even a hard-working dad needs to spend time with his kids. Lots of time.

Sadly, the average American dad spends only fourteen minutes a day with his children. I am convinced that one of the ways children take on the image of their fathers is by gazing into their faces. That requires eye contact, which means that fathers need to engage their children face to face. Fathers should talk to their children. They should teach them and play with them.

Fathers should also worship with their children. The best way to teach children that knowing Jesus Christ is the most important thing in the world is to treat it as the most important thing in the world. That means spending time in family worship. There are plenty of ways for families to worship together. But the key is for the father to be the worship leader, not in a pushy or legalistic way, but as the natural outflow of his heart's desire.

Most fathers can do a lot better in most of the areas I have mentioned. But start somewhere. Keep in mind what a good father does and, more importantly, what God he serves.

17

GROWING KIDS THE EZZO WAY

*W*hen Gary and Anne Marie Ezzo first taught a class on Christian parenting in 1984, 12 parents attended. The next time they offered the class, 160 parents signed up to take it, and the Ezzos were off and running. Soon they were publishing books, selling videos, and hosting conferences for parents all over America. Growing Families International now boasts that it has trained half a million parents worldwide.

The main Ezzo curriculum is called *Growing Kids God's Way*. The Ezzos also sell two different books for new parents—an explicitly Christian book called *Preparation for Parenting* and a hot-selling book for the secular audience called *On Becoming Babywise*.[1]

I mention these materials in order to give some guidance. I heard of one church in the Western United States that became polarized into two factions. The Ezzo parents were evangelists for *Growing Kids God's Way*. They suspected that their counterparts were not committed to biblical parenting. For their part, the anti-Ezzo parents made snide remarks about the way the Ezzo parents were rearing their children.

Having read much of the training material myself, I am happy enough for Christian parents to read the Ezzo books, although I cannot give them an unqualified endorsement.

Before I mention some of the limitations of growing kids the Ezzo way, let me mention some of the strengths. *Growing Kids God's Way:*

- takes the God-given responsibility of parenting seriously,
- recognizes that children are sinful by nature,
- has the goal of producing children who love and serve the Lord from the heart,
- contains plenty of practical wisdom for daily family life,
- stresses the necessity of fathers establishing intimacy with their children,
- more or less correctly explains the difference between spanking as it is generally practiced and the biblical concept of chastisement (see Prov. 23:13–14).

One of the more controversial principles the Ezzos espouse is that family life should be parent-centered. All other family relationships are secondary to the marriage. Rather than always catering to the whims of their children, Christian parents should help them adapt their desires to the needs of the family.

What is right about this emphasis is that the relationship between a mother and a father ought to be the strength of a family. Nothing gives more security to children than knowing that their dad loves their mom, and always will. It is also true that it is a mistake for parents to idolize their children.

One potential weakness of a parent-centered approach, however, is its failure to recognize the degree to which parenting is sacrifice. Parents need to be reminded of this because their natural inclination is to be selfish. But children do not exist for the sake of their parents; quite the opposite (2 Cor. 12:14). So parents should be quick to meet their children's real needs, which are different from mere desires. "Which of you," Jesus asks, "if his son asks for bread, will give him a stone? Or if he asks for a fish, will give him a snake?" (Matt. 7:9–10).

Another potential danger is treating these or other parenting manuals as more than they are. Many Christians are looking for guidance about how to become godly parents. The best way to get such guidance is to seek the counsel of Christian parents whose children are admired. Reading a variety of good books about parenting can also be helpful. The temptation, though, is to trust some parenting technique for salvation.

With that in mind, the title of the main Ezzo manual is a little alarming: *Growing Kids God's Way*, as if this were the only biblical way to parent. But one of the most important things the Ezzos say comes near the beginning of that book:

> The basis for *Growing Kids God's Way* is a theological framework and the experience and research that we have acquired in the process of successfully rearing our own children. However, it is only one perspective assisting parents in their responsibilities. While biblical doctrine provides the basis for parental standards, Scripture has very few specific mandates for practical applications.[2]

It makes me uneasy when the Ezzos claim to be "successful parents," since the truly outstanding parents I know would never make that claim. Their main point, however, is extremely helpful: the Bible contains very few rules for parenting. Therefore, most practical instruction about family life needs to be recognized for what it is: advice. Figuring out the difference between good advice and bad advice is where wisdom comes in. I suspect

that much of the controversy about growing kids the Ezzo way arises because some parents end up giving the materials almost biblical status.

One other area in which the Ezzos may lead parents astray is in their
use of the Bible. For example, they caution parents not to pick up their infants every time they cry. Instead, they should learn to identify different
kinds of cries; not every whimper demands a cuddle. Fair enough. However, in support of letting children cry themselves to sleep, the Ezzos say,
"God is not sitting on His throne waiting to jump up at our every cry, trying to prove that He loves us." They also cite Matthew 27:46: "My God,
my God, why have you forsaken me?" Using that verse to determine when
to pick up a crying baby is not merely nonsense; it is sacrilege.

The point is that reading books on parenting requires wisdom. If there
were only one way to rear godly children, God would have told us what it
is. Since he hasn't, Christian parents must work out this area of life, like all
others, with prayer and trembling (see Phil. 2:12).

18

SCM Seeks SCF
for LTR

*T*he title of this chapter comes from the sometimes bizarre lingo of Christian personals: "Single Christian male seeks single Christian female for long-term relationship." Or in adspeak, "SCM seeks SCF for LTR."

I began thinking about Christian personals when the *Christian Dating Newsletter* arrived in the church mail. It caught my attention for two reasons. First, unlike most ministries, the sponsor can be accessed only via a 1–900 telephone number, at two dollars per minute. But the newsletter also caught my attention because, much to my surprise, it featured lengthy promotional material for City Light, the singles ministry of Philadelphia's

Tenth Presbyterian Church. Apparently City Light had become renowned throughout the Delaware Valley as *the* place to meet eligible Christians on Friday nights.

The arrival of the newsletter raised a question. Should single Christians run personal ads? What does the Bible say about how to find a mate, or about whether it is even right to look for one in the first place?

The Bible does not tell contemporary Christians how to find a spouse. Consider the biblical examples. There was Isaac, who married Rebekah based on her ability to draw water for camels (Gen. 24). There was Jacob, who was able to choose a wife for himself but had to work fourteen years to get her (Gen. 29). Then there were the prophets: Hosea was told to marry a prostitute (Hos. 1). All in all, there is not much here to go on. It is safe to conclude that God gives people the freedom to meet and to marry in many different ways.

God's providence over marriage is infinite in its variety. Little did I suspect, when I saw Lisa Maxwell sitting on the edge of a couch during orientation week at Wheaton College, that my life would never be the same. But every couple meets in a different way. I once performed a wedding for a couple who first met in New York for a blind date set up by friends in Korea, halfway around the world. The providence of God extends even to dating newsletters, which, no doubt, have produced some happy marriages.

One thing Christian personals acknowledge is the importance of sexual purity. A quick glance at the personals in any city newspaper is enough to show how raunchy they are. But Christian ads have a different tone. They often feature evangelical vocabulary like "Spirit-filled" or "serious about the Lord." They recognize that there is more to a relationship than sex.

This is so important that it probably needs to be repeated. The Bible forbids sexual intimacy outside of marriage (see 1 Cor. 6:12–20). Period. If a couple asks, "Where is the line?" they have probably crossed it already. Call it what you will, but most physical intimacy between a man and a woman is foreplay, which is why couples often end up breaking the boundaries they set. I encourage single men, especially, to seek counsel from godly husbands about how to maintain sexual purity in a relationship.

Another thing Christian personals acknowledge is that Christians should not date non-Christians. Period. The only legitimate purpose for dating is courtship. But Christians may marry only other Christians (2 Cor. 6:14); therefore, they should date only other Christians. Since the Bible gives relatively few explicit instructions about love and romance, we must be all the more careful to obey the ones it does give.

If I am starting to sound like I recommend Christian personals, I don't intend to. The fact that they occasionally lead to marriage says more about God's providence than about human wisdom.

For one thing, like their secular counterparts, many Christian personals focus on appearance. Information about height, weight, and hair color comes up frequently, as do terms like "attractive" or "physically fit." Our culture places far too much importance on physical beauty, which, after all, is only temporary. And we place too little value on basic friendship, which is foundational to a happy marriage.

Another problem with many Christian personals is the desire that lies behind them. One ad came right to the point: "Seeking Mate." Yet the Bible does not say whether or not God even wants us to be married.

Sometimes I wish the Bible spelled things out more clearly. I wish it came with a personal appendix, a sort of Epistle to Philip. As I envision it, God's letter to me would contain hints, guidelines, and especially prophecies that pertained uniquely and explicitly to the events of my life.

In his wisdom, God has not revealed information about things like our future marital status. But one thing God's Word does reveal is that God wants us to accept our present circumstances. He wants us to be content. Whether we are married or single, at this moment, this is God's best plan for our lives.

Paige Benton, who does campus ministry for the Presbyterian Church in America, has a refreshing approach to singleness. She writes:

I long to be married. My younger sister got married two months ago. She now has an adoring husband, a beautiful home, a whirlpool bathtub, and all-new Corningware. Is God being any less good to me than he is to her? The answer is a resounding NO. God will not be less good to me because God cannot be less good to me. It is a cosmic impossibility for God to shortchange any of his children. . . . If he fluctuated one quark in his goodness he would cease to be God. . . . I am not single because I am too spiritually unstable to possibly deserve a husband, nor because I am too spiritually mature to possibly need one. I am single because God is so abundantly good to me, because this is his best for me.[1]

That is a wonderful attitude for anyone—married or single—to take about life. Too often we want to bend God to our desires rather than allowing God to shape our desires to match his plans. My present circumstances are God's best for me. He is doing what he is doing in my life because, ultimately, he loves me. And that is the long-term relationship that matters most of all.

19

WHAT SHOULD WE DO
WITH MOTHER?

*W*hat should we do with Mother, or Father? Anyone who has ever cared for an aged parent can testify that this is one of the most difficult questions a child ever has to face. For so many years, it was our parents' responsibility to care for us. They helped and advised us; on occasion, they tried to tell us what to do. But the situation gradually changed, until finally it seemed as if the roles were reversed. Eventually most children end up parenting their parents, caring for them and making decisions on their behalf. This is not an easy adjustment to make—either for parents or their children.

Some of the difficult decisions are financial and involve a baffling encounter with hospital bills, insurance forms, and government papers. What is the best use of a parent's limited resources? Who should decide how to use them? Other decisions are medical. How much should Mother be told about her condition? What's the best course of treatment? Should the family get a second opinion? Then at the end come the most difficult medical decisions of all, ones that involve equipment like artificial respirators.

Before that time comes, many of the most difficult decisions surround a parent's living situation. At what point is Mother unable to live on her own? And when she reaches the point when independence must be exchanged for dependence, where should she go? She could move home to live with her children, but are they prepared for the stress that this will cause the family? Or perhaps it would be better for Mother to live in a nursing home. But is she willing to go? If she is, how well will she be cared for? Will her dignity be preserved, as well as her safety?

Meanwhile, as children struggle with these issues, their mothers and fathers continue to grow ever older. The family goes through a grieving process as they witness the deterioration of physical and perhaps mental capacity. This process can go on for decades, and during the long good-bye, many children discover that they were better prepared for their parents to die than to keep on living. In some mysterious way, as our parents prepare for eternity, God will sanctify our tears. But the Bible is right when it says that these years have "no pleasure in them" (Eccles. 12:1).

If those are the questions, then what are the answers? The Bible says relatively little about how to care for an aged parent. The basic principle is "Honor your father and your mother" (Ex. 20:12). That commandment lasts for a lifetime, but it seems short on specifics. Furthermore, what it demands from a child changes according to the various stages of life. The nearer death seems to approach, the harder it is to know exactly what it means to honor one's parents.

What is obvious is that God gives children the responsibility to care for their parents in old age. Remember, "if anyone does not provide for his relatives, and especially for his immediate family, he has denied the faith and is worse than an unbeliever" (1 Tim. 5:8). Yet far too many elderly people are left to fend for themselves. One doctor commented, "One of the issues I see as I treat a large geriatric population is the lack of family involvement either as a result of 'too-busy' family members, no family members nearby, or lack of family infrastructure." The Bible's answer to this problem is that Christian children should care for their parents.

This does not necessarily mean that children always must care for their parents in their homes. Sometimes there are compelling reasons for an aged parent to live somewhere else. Depending on the situation, nursing home or hospice care may be advisable or even necessary. However, a child's first impulse should be to care for his parents as directly as possible. Far too many elderly Americans live in nursing homes as a matter of neglectful convenience.

If Mother does live in a nursing home, be sure to stay closely involved. Visit her as often as possible. Get to know the nursing home staff personally, visiting or making telephone calls at different times of the day. Ask friendly but probing questions about her care.

Remember also to rely on the help of the extended family, the church. Whenever I visit a nursing home, I am reminded of the value of being a church member. Our church makes a regular practice of holding services at area nursing homes, but we attempt to take special care of our members. Toward that end, we maintain a list of church members who live in nursing homes or are otherwise unable to leave their homes. Besides praying for them, we ask each parish council to care faithfully for the shut-ins in their part of the city. As parents grow older, be sure to stay in touch with their local church family, which can provide friendship and spiritual care. Jesus set the example when he committed his mother Mary to the care of his friend John (John 19:25–27).

When it comes to difficult medical issues, one way to honor our parents is by telling them the truth. Admittedly, there are many occasions when the truth will not be welcome. Old age is a time of life when most of the news seems to be bad news, especially where the body is concerned. But often children must be the ones who face up to the hard realities and care enough to say what needs to be said. It is our responsibility as Christian children to tell the truth and also to find the most loving way to say it.

Some Christians have not yet had to care for an aging parent. For some of us, these issues seem decades away. However, it is never too early to talk about them. Some medical decisions will be easier to make if families have discussed them in advance. It is often prudent for parents to give their children durable power of attorney for medical and financial matters.

Those who are already struggling with these issues will need more help than these brief comments can provide. Each situation is different and each requires fervent prayer and personal spiritual conference. But know this: every effort to take care of an aging parent is pleasing to God. And no matter how distressing and perplexing our situation becomes, he is sufficient, for his power is "made perfect in weakness" (2 Cor. 12:9a).

20

WHEN THE ALMOND TREE BLOSSOMS

*S*he was getting old. At the time I think she was eighty-eight, but it was hard to keep track. She lived far away in a home in Pella, Iowa, the city of refuge.

I was awakened by the Spirit to pray for my grandmother Eva in the middle of the night. I later learned why Grandma needed my prayers. She had fallen out of bed and injured herself. Too weak to climb back into bed, she lay in the dark for an hour before crawling to the door to call for help.

After that Grandma suffered a stroke. She lost some of her movement and some of her ability to reason. When she could no longer take care of her needs, she was not allowed to return to her former home. That was hard, and it made some of her nurses—and even her own children—seem to her like adversaries. This was frightening for her and distressing for everyone else.

It is hard to watch someone grow old. It must be even harder for the person who is growing old. The writer of Ecclesiastes composed a poem about aging. It is a beautiful, but melancholy, poem:

> Remember your Creator
>   in the days of your youth,
> before the days of trouble come
>   and the years approach when you will say,
>   "I find no pleasure in them"—
> before the sun and the light
>   and the moon and the stars grow dark,
>   and the clouds return after the rain;
> when the keepers of the house tremble,
>   and the strong men stoop,
> when the grinders cease because they are few,
>   and those looking through the windows grow dim;
> when the doors to the street are closed
>   and the sound of grinding fades;
> when men rise up at the sound of birds,
>   but all their songs grow faint;
> when men are afraid of heights
>   and of dangers in the streets;
> when the almond tree blossoms
>   and the grasshopper drags himself along
>   and desire no longer is stirred.
> Then man goes to his eternal home
>   and mourners go about the streets. (Eccles. 12:1–5)

Everything the Bible describes so vividly came to pass in my grandmother's old age. She had few pleasures. Her hands were unsteady, and her back was stooped. She lost her teeth, and her eyes grew dim. She woke up with the birds, or earlier, but she could not hear them very well. When she went out she was in danger of falling. Her hair was white, like the almond tree in springtime. The poet would say that her desire no longer stirred. She told me she didn't have much "pep." Not long afterwards she went to her eternal rest, and the mourners gathered in the streets.

As I watched my grandmother grow old I learned at least two lessons about the way God cares for the elderly. The first is that godly children are one of life's greatest blessings. Proverbs states that "children's children are a crown to the aged" (Prov. 17:6a), which is especially true when those children belong to the Lord. My grandmother went one generation better than the proverb. She was crowned with her children's children's children. Whenever she wrote to me she asked how her great-grandchildren were doing. In my mind I could see her lifting their pictures from her desk and praising God for her reward.

The greater blessing God gave my grandmother was the gift of himself. My grandmother had a special friendship with God. She was a great woman of prayer. She prayed for her church and her family by day and by night. She interceded for my preaching so fervently that sometimes I wondered if my ministry could survive the loss of her prayers.

I believe that some of the most valuable work in the kingdom of God is done by men and women like my grandmother. Often the elderly have more time to devote to the life of prayer. They can spend less time doing and more time praying. Furthermore, older Christians have strong confidence in the power of prayer and long experience in the need for prayer. They also have a good idea what to pray about. It only makes sense for the most valuable and difficult Christian work—namely, intercession—to be undertaken by those with the greatest spiritual maturity.

The fruit of a life of prayer is the closest intimacy with God. At the end my grandmother had less of almost everything in her life—less food, less fellowship, less furniture. But she had more of God than ever. "You know," she would say to me, "it is as if God lives with me right here in this room, and I know he does."

This testimony should be an encouragement to the aged. The Bible is honest about the hardships of growing old, but it is also generous in the honor it gives to the elderly. The Lord blesses older saints, and the best blessing of all is the gift of himself. For the sake of the church, every older Christian should strive to become a man or woman of prayer.

This also poses a challenge to the young. The poem in Ecclesiastes is about old age, but it is mainly for the young. It reminds us to remember our Creator in the days of our youth. It is very difficult for an aged sinner to come to Christ in faith. An old mind finds it hard to understand the truth, and an old heart can be a hard heart. It would be much better to become a friend of Christ now. Then there would be time for a relationship with God to grow into the kind of friendship my grandmother enjoyed. After all, old friends make the best friends.

PART 4

THE ARTS

Nor am I of the opinion that through the Gospel all art should be cast to the ground and should perish, as some misled religious people claim. But I want to see all the arts, especially music, used in the service of Him who has given and created them. I therefore pray that every pious Christian will agree with this, and if God has given him equal or greater gifts, will lend his aid.

—MARTIN LUTHER

*C*hristians tend to be suspicious about the arts. There are some good reasons for this. One is that images easily lend themselves to idolatry. Although God's command not to make graven images (Ex. 20:4–6) has more to do with worship than with art, it is nevertheless significant that God forbids the crafting of images. Artists trade in images, and the image has a way of displacing the word.

Another reason Christians are suspicious is because so much modern and postmodern art wallows in depravity. Anyone who doubts this should visit the senior exhibition of virtually any art school in the country. Many contemporary artists are hostile to the Christian way of looking at the world.

On the other side, artists have plenty of reasons to be suspicious about the church. Christians have often showed artists the door, or even shoved them out. On occasion, they have smashed their artwork for good measure. Then there is the indisputable fact that Christians have produced a great deal of bad art in the name of Christ. Just because an artist happens to be a Christian doesn't mean that his or her art is any good.

All of this suspicion is not only unfortunate but also unnecessary. Christianity has something important to say to the artist because it places art in its proper context. The Christian view of art begins with the claim that God is an artist—the Artist, in fact. Our Father has revealed his artistry in everything he has made. He also makes aesthetic judgments. The first thing that God observed about the world he made was that it was very good, thus establishing a normative standard for the arts.

There is also something redemptive about God's artistry. In making the world he brought order out of chaos, turning what was disordered into something harmonious and beautiful. He is not finished yet, either. God has promised that one day he will make a new heaven and a new earth (2 Peter 3:13). It will be marvelous beyond imagination, for "no eye has seen, no ear has heard, no mind has conceived what God has prepared for those who love him" (1 Cor. 2:9).

Artists also have something important to say to the church. Art is still a leading cultural indicator. Today's artwork becomes tomorrow's world-view. For this reason, it is important for Christians to study and discuss art in all its various forms.

The essays that follow come from an amateur, not an expert. Their importance—if they are important—lies not in the subjects they address or in the judgments they contain but in the underlying principles they present for a Christian view of art.

21

THE SERIOUS BUSINESS

OF HEAVEN

*F*riday, January 31, 1997, was the bicentennial of the birth of the Austrian composer Franz Schubert (1797–1828). Around that time it was virtually impossible to go to a classical concert anywhere in Philadelphia without hearing Schubert. Schubert was being played by The Philadelphia Orchestra and The Curtis Institute, as well as in various restaurants around Rittenhouse Square. The 1700 block of Latimer Street was even renamed Schubert Alley.

I celebrated Schubert's birth with an evening of music at the Church of the Holy Trinity. The program featured a pleasing variety of piano solos, chamber music, and *lieder*, including the instrumental and vocal versions of Schubert's famous *Trout Quintet* (Quintet for Piano and Strings in A Major, D.667). The concert closed with the audience joining in a performance of Schubert's short Mass no. 2 in G Major (D.167).

The celebration continued throughout the year, with plenty of Schubert to play. Although he died at the age of thirty-one, his total musical output exceeds that of Mozart and Beethoven combined. More than two hundred years after his birth, Schubert still receives acclaim as a composer of the first rank.

Schubert's compositions have something to teach us about the joy of music in the Christian life. C. S. Lewis once observed that "joy is the serious business of heaven."[1] If Lewis is right, then one way to prepare for our eternal occupation is to play and listen to music. It is in music, most of all, that the soul anticipates the joy of life with God.

Schubert was not always joyful. For the last decade of his life he suffered from the debilitating effects of syphilis. The misery of his illness is captured in a letter he wrote to a friend in 1824:

> In a word, I feel myself to be the most unhappy and wretched creature in the world. Imagine a man whose health will never be right again, and who, in sheer despair over this, ever makes things worse and worse, instead of better; imagine a man, I say, whose most brilliant hopes have perished, to whom the felicity of love and friendship have nothing to offer but pain.[2]

It seems unlikely that Schubert ever took his sufferings to the Lord. He was not known for his godliness, and he rarely acknowledged that his musical gifts came from God. Although he wrote many works to be performed in church, Schubert's real passion was reserved for secular songs, for opera and orchestral music. A friend once wrote to him, "Credo in unum Deum"—"I believe in one God." But then he admitted, "I know very well that you do not." Schubert's attitude toward Jesus Christ is perhaps summed up in his condescending words about one of his brothers: "He probably still keeps crawling to the cross."

If Schubert did not praise God for his music, many others have done so. His first teacher said, "If I wished to instruct him in anything fresh, he already knew it. Consequently I gave him no actual tuition but merely conversed with him and watched him with silent astonishment." When he went to the imperial court in Vienna as a choirboy, one of his teachers exclaimed, "He has learnt everything from God, that lad." Beethoven was given some of Schubert's songs to study while he was on his deathbed. He was so moved that he said, "Truly in Schubert there is a divine spark."[3]

Wolfgang Sawallisch, the conductor of the Philadelphia Orchestra, said much the same thing. He tried to explain Schubert's "gentle musical power," the almost "magical" quality of his music. But Sawallisch was unable to account for Schubert's gift, unless perhaps the lines on his musical score had fallen "down from the heavens."

Beautiful music is always a gift from God. God conducted the first choir in the universe, "while the morning stars sang together and all the angels shouted for joy" (Job 38:7). The Bible is careful to record the name of the first great musician in human history, Jubal: "he was the father of all who play the harp and flute" (Gen. 4:21). Music is part of God's common grace, one of the blessings he has poured out on humanity in general, through men and women such as Franz Schubert.

Schubertiade are concerts that began during Schubert's lifetime when friends would gather in his home to sing, dance, read poetry, and perform new music. They were occasions of joy and celebration.

It is good for Christians to celebrate *Schubertiade*. Enjoying music is one of the best ways to practice "the serious business of heaven." But when we play or listen to Schubert we are not simply praising the gift of his music; we are praising the Giver of all good gifts. Proper *Schubertiade* are celebrations of the God who has made us music makers. This is why, when the Bible refers to music, it speaks most often of music "to the LORD" or "to our God" (e.g., Ps. 27:6, 147:7). Music is properly offered in praise to God. It should always be listened to or played to his glory.

There was glory—and joy—in the music we sang in Philadelphia on the night of Schubert's bicentennial. The *Kyrie* was hushed, contemplative: "Lord, have mercy. Lord, have mercy." But then the orchestra leaped and skipped into the *Gloria*, with the choir rushing to keep pace. "Gloria in excelsis Deo!" "Glory to God in the highest!"

22

THANKS FOR
MENDELSSOHN

*N*ovember 1997 marked 150 years since the death of one of the greatest composers, Felix Mendelssohn-Bartholdy (1809–1847). Mendelssohn's symphonies, concertos, oratorios, and chamber works made him wildly popular during his lifetime. Yet for many years after his death, his musical reputation went into decline. Among the German intelligentsia, he had two marks against him: he was a Jew, which offended musicians like Richard Wagner, and he was a Christian, which offended philosophers like Ludwig Wittgenstein.

Mendelssohn was born into an unusually gifted family. His sister Fanny possibly was as accomplished a pianist as he was. His grandfather Moses was a noted philosopher. His father Abraham was a prominent banker who converted to the Christian faith. Upon his conversion he changed the family name to Mendelssohn-Bartholdy.

Felix Mendelssohn was well known for his Christian convictions. His sacred compositions reflect his careful study of Scripture. All his works reflect his conviction that "every genre in the arts is first elevated above the level of craft when it devotes itself by means of the greatest possible technical perfection to a purely spiritual purpose for the expression of a higher idea."[1] It is significant that Mendelssohn signed his manuscripts with the prayer, "Let it succeed, God."

One of Mendelssohn's most important choral works is his Symphony no. 2 in B-flat Major, op. 52, 1840, also called *Lobgesang*, or "Hymn of Praise." Like many of Mendelssohn's compositions, the second symphony has profound theological significance. The work was written to mark the four-hundredth anniversary of the Gutenberg Bible. It begins with a long orchestral movement, more than a third of the length of the symphony. The melody is well developed, yet something seems to be missing.

Then the choir is introduced, and we hear what was absent. As many as a hundred voices sing, "Alles, was Odem hat, lobe den Herrn!" ("All that hath breath praise the Lord!"). What was missing was breath coming from lungs and passing over vocal chords to produce music made by human voices.

In the whole creation, only human beings have received the very breath of God. In the history of creation we read that "the LORD God formed man from the dust of the ground and breathed into his nostrils the breath of life, and man became a living being" (Gen. 2:7). The praise of God is not complete until everything that has breath gives him praise, especially human beings made in his image.

In case we miss the point, Mendelssohn, who selected all of the biblical texts for *Lobgesang*, has the choir go on to sing:

> Praise the Lord with stringed instruments,
> extol him with your song,
> and let all flesh praise his holy name.
> All that hath breath praise the Lord.

This is exactly what happens in the symphony. Voice is added to string in praise of God. Without the choir, the "Hymn of Praise" would be incomplete. But when the choir bursts into song everything that has breath praises the Lord.

It is good to praise God as Creator, but it is not enough. We must also praise him as Redeemer, so a soloist steps forward to testify that God has saved us as well as made us:

Tell it forth, ye that are redeemed,
that he freed you from your distress,
from dire affliction, shame, and bondage,
ye who sat in the power of darkness,
all whom he hath redeemed from distress.
Tell it forth! Give thanks to him and proclaim his goodness!

Mendelssohn had experienced the grace of God. But he also understood that every life is touched by grief and sorrow, especially the Christian life. So the *Lobgesang* passes through a dark night of the soul. In anguish the believer tells how

The bonds of death had closed around us,
the sorrows of hell prevented us.
We wandered in darkness.

He wonders when, or even if, his sufferings will ever end. Over and over he cries out, "Watchman, will the night soon pass?"

Then a soprano appears, like an angel, somewhere high in the auditorium to sing words of peace and benediction: "The night has departed" ("Die Nacht ist vergangen"). The light of the glory of God shines to turn darkness into light.

It is at this point that the full choir again gives thanks to God. The choir expresses the simple harmonies of the chorale, the kind of hymn one would hear in church. The point is that once the believer has passed through trial, he rejoins his brothers and sisters to praise God.

What the choir sings has become one of the most familiar thanksgiving hymns. The first line of the hymn, which was originally composed by Johann Crüger (1647), is "Now thank we all our God." Here is a different translation:

Let all men praise the Lord,
In worship lowly bending,
On his most holy word;
Redeem'd from woe depending,
He gracious is, and just,
From childhood us doth lead,
On him we place our trust,
And hope in time of need.

Glory and praise to God
The Father, Son, be given,
And to the Holy Ghost,
On high enthron'd in heaven,
Praise to the triune God,
With pow'rful arm and strong,
He changeth night to day.
Praise him with grateful song.

Lobgesang is the story of every Christian. First, we recognize God as Creator. Then we use our breath to praise Christ as Redeemer. We pass through various tribulations, wondering if we will ever see the morning light. But God proves faithful, and we offer him a "Hymn of Praise" all over again. So give thanks to God for music, for Mendelssohn, for salvation in Christ, for care in suffering, and for watchful providence from earliest days until this very moment.[2]

23

CÉZANNE

*W*hen the famous Cézanne exhibition came to Philadelphia in the summer of 1998, I went to see it. Although I have no special expertise in the field of art, a major exhibition provides a good opportunity to view culture from the Christian perspective. What can we learn from Cézanne?

Paul Cézanne (1839–1906) is widely regarded as the greatest painter of the nineteenth century. The exhibition of his paintings in Philadelphia and other major cities was touted as one of the great art shows of all time. It included nearly two hundred of the artist's works. But what did it all mean?

We learn some of the basic principles for a biblical critique of culture from the apostle Paul: "Finally, brothers, whatever is true, whatever is noble, whatever is right, whatever is pure, whatever is lovely, whatever is admirable—if anything is excellent or praiseworthy—think about such things" (Phil. 4:8).

By this standard, Cézanne painted many excellent and praiseworthy paintings, and the effect of seeing so many of them at once was awe-inspiring. They were arranged in more or less chronological order, so it was easy to see the progress of Cézanne's artistry. The difference between his early paintings and his mature work is striking. Cézanne also painted many lovely things, like the passionate greens and golds of his landscapes of Mont Sainte-Victoire or the solid structure and the luminous coloration of the apples in his still lifes.

But what about truth? Are Cézanne's paintings true? More particularly, are his paintings of human beings true to the nature of persons as God has created them? My opinion, which not all Christians will share, is that Cézanne's presentation of the person is deeply disturbing. Most of his portraits evoke neither joy, nor love, nor even pity.

Consider the figures in Cézanne's *The Card Players* (1890–1892). The painting depicts two men, seated at a table, playing cards. The figures are hunched over, their limbs are awkward, and their heads are almost too small for their bodies. Both men are withdrawn, isolated, and introspective. They are so absorbed in their own affairs that there is little interaction between them. In fact, they are holding their cards so close to one another that they have not left one another enough space to play their hands.

There is a similar sense of detachment in Cézanne's *Young Girl at the Piano—Overture to Tannhauser* (1869). In the painting one young girl sits on the sofa and sews while another—her back turned—is playing the piano. The girls are almost but not quite part of the landscape, as if they are inanimate objects. For Cézanne, the painting is more important than the person. In the words of one critic, "the human figure presented mainly pictorial and architectural problems for Cézanne; he could not see its spiritual dimension—its role as the subject and object of love."[1]

That judgment seemed to be confirmed by the retrospective. It could even be applied to Cézanne's crowning achievement: *The Large Bathers*

(1906). The exhibition was arranged so as to give Cézanne's *Large Bathers* the attention it deserves. The painting stood alone on a large wall, confronting the observer walking out of the main gallery. Because of its monumental size and the delicate beauty of its colors, *The Large Bathers* has to be seen in person to be fully appreciated.

The bathers are awkward, clumsy, ungainly, even distorted. They are obviously females, but they are not feminine. They are painted, I think, without a real appreciation for the beauty of the human figure or a love for the human person as a bearer of the divine image. Once again, the figures in Cézanne's painting are isolated. They are not engaged in play, or lively conversation, or even bathing. Instead, they gaze inward, preoccupied with their own thoughts.

It is often pointed out that Cézanne exercised a seminal influence on modern art, bridging the gap between Impressionism and Cubism. The great modern artist Pablo Picasso (1881–1973) called him "the father of us all." It is instructive, therefore, to compare Cézanne's *Large Bathers* with Picasso's painting *Les Demoiselles d'Avignon* (1907). Picasso's damsels are disjointed, grotesque, and even hideous. Where Cézanne saw the isolation of the person, Picasso saw the fragmentation of the person. Where Cézanne tried to redefine the person, Picasso tried to destroy the person.

Although Cézanne cannot be blamed for everything his artistic children have done, he is at least responsible for the ideas that made their art possible. Are his paintings true? They do give some insight into the loneliness of human depravity. Cézanne's paintings are not true to the way God made human beings, but they do tell us something true about what human beings have made of themselves. What they lack is the note of redemption, which shows what human beings can become, by the grace of God.

24

FACE TO FACE: VAN GOGH'S PORTRAITURE

*F*ace to Face" was the subtitle of an art exhibition at the Philadelphia Museum of Art, the first devoted exclusively to the portraiture of the Dutch master Vincent van Gogh (1853–1890). The show included several self-portraits. Hence its full title: "Van Gogh: Face to Face."

The exhibition was of interest to Christians because it brought viewers face to face with the human condition. A gallery full of portraits cannot help but make some kind of statement about what it means to be a human being. That is especially true of the portraits of Vincent van Gogh, who wrote,

> That which excites me the most . . . is the portrait, the modern portrait. . . . I should like to do portraits which will appear as revelations to people in a hundred years' time. . . . I am not trying to achieve this by photographic likeness but by rendering our impassioned expressions, by using our modern knowledge and appreciation of color as a means of rendering and exalting character.[1]

In other words, the artist's goal was not to reproduce the outward appearance of his subjects but to communicate their inward essence. He tried to produce "portraiture with the soul of the model in it."

Most of van Gogh's models were ordinary people: men from the old people's home, gardeners, soldiers, peasants, and even prostitutes. Then there are the famous portraits of the Roulin family: a postman, his wife, and their three children. One reason van Gogh painted common people was because he could not afford to pay professional models. But it was also a matter of principle: he believed that poor people were the proper focus of modern art. Since they lack the trappings of power and prosperity, what shows through in their portraits is their humanity—and nothing else.

Nearly all of van Gogh's subjects have a quiet dignity. The artist recognized that there was something Godlike about every person. He wrote, "I want to paint men and women with that something of the eternal which the halo used to symbolize, and which we seek to convey by actual radiance and vibration of our coloring." Yet for all their dignity, the people in van Gogh's paintings are also smudged by sin and toil. This too was part of the painter's purpose: "I want to make drawings that touch some people. . . . What I want to express . . . isn't anything sentimental or melancholy, but deep anguish."

By God's common grace, van Gogh's portraits show what it means to be a person made in God's image and living in a fallen world. Like all true art, his portraits speak the truth about the human condition. They show the dignity and frailty of humanity.

One might contrast van Gogh's portraits with the landscapes of

Thomas Kinkade, now available at many shopping malls. Although Kinkade is a Christian, there is a sense in which his paintings are somewhat less than fully Christian because, by the artist's own admission, they "portray a world without the fall," and thus they cannot point to the possibility of redemption.

What is surprising about all this is that as far as anyone knows, Vincent van Gogh repudiated the Christian faith. Despite being reared in a Christian home—the home, in fact, of a minister in the Dutch Reformed Church—and despite having some kind of conversion experience, the artist abandoned the church and never returned.

During early adulthood, for about four years, van Gogh was outspoken in his Christian commitment. His personal letters from this time are full of biblical quotations. He described being born again to eternal life as "a gift of God, a work of God—and of God alone." Vincent even prepared for the gospel ministry, serving first as a Bible teacher at a church in England. After his first sermon, he wrote, "I felt like someone who had risen from a dark vault underground into the kind light of day when I stood at the pulpit, and it is a glorious thought that from now on wherever I go, I shall preach the gospel." From there van Gogh went to seminary, before going on to become a missionary to Belgian coal miners.

Yet he grew disillusioned with the church, and especially with the hypocrisy of the clergy. During the last decade of his life van Gogh said almost nothing about his personal relationship to Christ. Instead, he turned to his artwork, finding it to be "something which I can devote myself to heart and soul, and which inspires me and gives meaning to life."

Although van Gogh sought meaning in his art, he was often anxious and sometimes despairing, probably due to manic depression. In some of his final works—such as *The Pieta, The Resurrection of Lazarus,* or *At Eternity's Gate*—he seemed to be searching again for the God of his childhood. But the artist came to a tragic end, going out into a field and shooting himself. As he lay dying, he told his brother, "I did it for the good of everybody."

Even if van Gogh's final spiritual condition is uncertain, his tragic tale warns us against apostasy. Some who seem to have faith ultimately renounce their allegiance to Christ (e.g., Gal. 5:4; 1 Tim. 1:19–20; 1 John 2:19). But it would be a mistake to think—based on van Gogh's experience—that one must decide between being an artist and becoming a Christian. It is possible to be both. The real choice is between living for God's glory and living for your own. If you decide to live for your glory, then whether you are a minister or an artist, you will serve yourself. But if you live for God, then whatever you do will be for his glory, whether you are a preacher or a painter. The question is, What has God called *you* to do?

25

THE (NOT SO)
PEACEABLE KINGDOM

*E*dward Hicks (b. 1780) was a nineteenth-century artist who lived in Pennsylvania. Although he began his career as a sign painter, he later became a minister in the Society of Friends, more commonly known as the Quakers. Yet Hicks never lost his love for painting, and he continued to produce works of art until the end of his life.

The most unusual feature of Hicks's work is that nearly all his formal paintings were variations on a single theme: the peaceable kingdom. Typically, on the right side of these paintings there is a small child, standing with a group of animals. Often the child has his arm wrapped around a lion's neck. Nearby stands an ox, and perhaps a bear or a wolf. In the foreground a leopard lies down with a lamb. In many cases there is a group of Quakers on the left side of the painting, standing in the background, usually under a large oak tree.

These paintings are based on the Bible. This was partly because Edward Hicks wanted to persuade his contemporaries among the Quakers that it was permissible for Christians to be practicing artists. But Hicks also wanted to express his hope in the biblical promise of peace on earth. Thus the paintings are based on a text from the prophet Isaiah:

> The wolf will live with the lamb,
>   the leopard will lie down with the goat,
> the calf and the lion and the yearling together;
>   and a little child will lead them.
> The cow will feed with the bear,
>   their young will lie down together,
>   and the lion will eat straw like the ox.
> The infant will play near the hole of the cobra,
>   and the young child put his hand into the viper's nest.
>   (Isa. 11:6–8)

In the autumn of 1999 the Philadelphia Museum of Art sponsored a show of Hicks's work. It was the first time that so many of his "Peaceable Kingdoms" were displayed in one show. What the exhibit powerfully demonstrated was the artist's struggle to find peace on earth.

The earliest paintings (1816–1828) are the most peaceful. A printed border surrounds most of them, which is why they are usually referred to as the "Border Peaceable Kingdoms." Hicks drew on his experience as a sign painter to produce the lettering around these paintings, which reads:

> The wolf shall with the lambkin dwell in peace,
> His grim carnivorous nature then shall cease;
> The leopard with the harmless kid lay down,

and not one savage beast be seen to frown;
The lion and the calf shall forward move,
A little child shall lead them in love.
When MAN is moved and led by sov'reign grace,
To seek that state of everlasting PEACE.

The animals in the "Border Peaceable Kingdoms" are sweet and mild, without any trace of tension or anxiety. The child has his arm gently and lovingly draped around the lion's neck. The Quaker William Penn is in the background, standing on the banks of the Delaware, signing a peace treaty with the Lenape Indians.

The next set of paintings is more disturbing. These are the "Banner Peaceable Kingdoms" (1829–1832), so called because there is a banner of text wrapped around the human figures. There are many signs of disquiet. The leopard looks tense, uneasy. The child still has his hand around the lion's neck, but he is grasping a handful of mane, struggling to keep the beast in place. The human figures are starting to disperse, and there is an ominous cleft in the oak tree. This represents a division within the Society of Friends between the Hicksites and the Orthodox. The Hicksites, under the influence of Edward's cousin Elias, advocated a simple rural lifestyle and opposed the prosperity of Quakers who lived in the city. They also resisted the authority of Scripture and opposed having elders in the church. As a result of these differences, there was a sharp division in the Quaker fellowship.

By 1832, when he began to paint his "Middle Peaceable Kingdoms" (1832–1840), Hicks doubted whether reconciliation was possible. As a result, many of the animals look fierce, even sinister. The lion bares his teeth. In a sermon preached at Goose Creek, Virginia, Hicks explained his symbolism: each animal represented a different aspect of human nature. His point was that there is something beastly about us. "The animal, man," he said, "possesses the nature and propensities of all other animals."

By the time he painted his final series of paintings, called the "Late

Peaceable Kingdoms" (1840s), Hicks seemed to have abandoned his hopes for peace on earth. Some of the animals, especially the leopards, are in out-right conflict, fighting one another. They are no longer grouped tightly to-gether but are dispersed across the canvas, representing the disunity of humanity. It was during this time that Hicks wrote of his former hope that "I should live to see the society of Friends come together but . . . the rant-ing un[settled] spirit among friends together with the feebleness of my hold on life has disapated [sic] that hope." Hicks's growing sense of fatigue is expressed most clearly in his last "Peaceable Kingdom," in which the lion is hunched over in sheer exhaustion.

What do these paintings tell us about the meaning of life? Art always expresses a point of view about ultimate truth. What Hicks seemed to be saying is that God's peaceable kingdom cannot be established on this earth. Not yet, at any rate. His experience in a sinful church gradually replaced the idealism of his youth with a more realistic view of human nature.

It is doubtful whether Hicks ever discovered that true and lasting peace comes only through Jesus Christ. Early on, there were some signs that he did understand this. In one painting, the child holds a branch with a clus-ter of grapes. The branch is a reference to Christ, based on Isaiah 11:1: "A shoot will come up from the stump of Jesse; from his roots a Branch will bear fruit." The grapes on the branch represent the blood Christ shed on the cross. There is also a painting in which the banner of peace flows from Christ, who stands on a high mountain.

But these are only fleeting images, and they disappear in Hicks's later work. He seems to have lost sight of the true basis for peace, that through Jesus God has reconciled "to himself all things, whether things on earth or things in heaven, by making peace through his blood, shed on the cross" (Col. 1:20). If Hicks had understood this, he would have known that one day soon God will make good on his promise, for when Christ returns, the leopard will lie down with the lamb.

26

THE REVEREND
MR. BROCKLEHURST

*T*he movie is never as good as the book, right?
Not always.

For a Christian minister, the first long scene of Franco Zeffirelli's *Jane Eyre* is appalling. In the scene a horse-drawn carriage pulls up the drive of Gateshead Hall, a small country estate. Out steps a tall, dark man with grotesque features, bushy black eyebrows, and a menacing scowl. Those familiar with the iconography of the modern film already will have guessed the man's occupation. Anyone this diabolical must be a minister.

And so he is. As the frightful man stands at the door he is solemnly in-

troduced to the lady of the house as the Reverend Mr. Brocklehurst. After
the exchange of a few unpleasantries young Jane Eyre is brought into the
sitting room for his inspection. As it turns out, the Reverend Mr. Brocklehurst is the headmaster of Lowood School. Young Jane is being presented
to him as a candidate for matriculation. The poor girl is an orphan who has
the misfortune of living with an aunt and cousins who are trying to get rid
of her by packing her off to boarding school.

"Your name, little girl?" asks Rev. Brocklehurst as he begins the inqui-
sition.

"Jane Eyre, sir."

"Well, Jane Eyre, are you a good child?"

Jane hesitates, because she knows full well that she is not a "good
child." Yet it will hardly do to admit that she is a naughty little girl. Her
aunt intervenes, "Perhaps the less said on that subject the better, Mr.
Brocklehurst."

The minister then calls the orphan to stand in front of his chair. "Do
you know where the wicked go after death?" he asks threateningly.

"They go to hell," she replies.

"And what is hell? Can you tell me that?"

"A pit full of fire."

"And should you like to fall into that pit, and to be burning there for ever?"

"No, sir."

"What must you do to avoid it?"

This was a subject Jane had not covered in catechism, so she was on uncertain ground when she answered, "I must keep in good health, and not die."[1]

The threatening and abusive Mr. Brocklehurst embodies the law of
God without displaying the grace of the gospel. He is the kind of minister
parishioners hate to see on their doorstep. As the movie continues, he is
increasingly sanctimonious, hypocritical, vengeful, and violent.

"There's a lesson in this," I informed my wife on the way home, "about the way the secular media portray the clergy. Unless they are effeminate, ministers are always portrayed as child molesters or serial killers. It's not just that they are weak and irrelevant; they are downright evil." I was certain that Zeffirelli had made Brocklehurst into a caricature of the character in Brontë's novel.

I was wrong. A friend also went to see *Jane Eyre* and shared my desire to see how the book compared with the film. "The minister isn't as bad in the book as he is in the movie," she told me a few days later. "He's worse!" To my surprise, it turns out that the portrait of Mr. Brocklehurst in the Zeffirelli film is faithful to the Brontë novel. It was a good lesson in the importance of getting facts straight and not exaggerating the evils of contemporary culture.

It also means that Charlotte Brontë (1816–1854) has something to teach us about hypocrisy in the church. When *Jane Eyre* was published, some of its first readers were alarmed by its portrayal of Christianity. They displayed the kind of misguided zeal I displayed when I saw the film. In her preface to the second edition of *Jane Eyre*, Charlotte Brontë answered her critics. Apparently some readers had mistaken Brontë's portrayal of the Reverend Mr. Brocklehurst for an attack on Christianity, or even for an attack on Christ. This criticism had a harsh bite to it because the Brontë sisters were the daughters of an Anglican minister.

Brontë used her preface to explain that her real motives were to strengthen the church, not to undermine its ministry. She was not attacking Jesus Christ; she was attacking those who called themselves Christians but did not live for Christ. "Self-righteousness is not religion," Brontë observed. "To attack the first is not to assail the last. To pluck the mask from the face of the Pharisee, is not to lift an impious hand to the Crown of Thorns."[2]

This was an especially perceptive comment. Too often our outrage about the way Christians are portrayed in the secular media is prompted by our pride rather than by true zeal for the glory of Christ. We worry too much about what other people think of us. We are too quick to defend our righteousness, which is indefensible.

One of the values of *Jane Eyre*—the movie and the book—is that it plucks the mask from our faces. What we ought to see in the Reverend Mr. Brocklehurst is a little bit of ourselves, especially those of us who are ministers. Like Brocklehurst, many of us are more effective at preaching the law than we are at living by grace, and there is something diabolical about that, after all.

SCIENCE AND TECHNOLOGY

The illusion that mechanical progress means human improvement . . . alienates us from our own being and our own reality. . . . Technology was made for man, not man for technology. In losing touch with being and thus with God, we have fallen into a senseless idolatry of production and consumption for their own sakes.

—THOMAS MERTON

Recent decades have witnessed spectacular advances in science and technology. Discoveries that were scarcely imaginable half a century ago have now become commonplace. This is the age of atomic weapons and nuclear energy, heart transplants and designer drugs, computers and cell phones, space shuttles and superscooters. We have now entered what many analysts are calling the biotech century. The advances are rapid: cloning, stem-cell research, gene therapy, and molecule-sized computer chips. The list goes on and on.

What makes all these advances possible is that we are living in our Father's world. Using the talents that he has given, we are discovering and developing the possibilities inherent in his creation.

Many people assume that advances in ethics are able to keep pace with progress in science and technology. Nothing could be further from the truth. For one thing, scientists have a way of charging ahead without waiting to think through the ethical implications of their discoveries. They face tremendous pressure to be the first to discover or invent something new. By the time new techniques and technologies are available, it is almost too late for anyone to ask whether they are moral or even beneficial. Scientists generally appeal to the potential benefits of their discoveries, but usually little is said about their costs, especially to human dignity.

It should be emphasized that Christianity is not opposed to modern science. In fact, Christianity played a major role in its development. By clearly distinguishing between the Creator and his creation and by insisting that the universe is the product of intelligent design, the Bible provided the principles that make scientific investigation possible.

Although Christianity is not opposed to science, Christians are often compelled to speak words of caution. What we know about human depravity leads us to believe that science will be put to evil uses as well as good ones. We also know that human beings are not to be tampered with. A person is a sacred thing, made in the image of God. So as Christians we are willing to draw boundaries, to say that there are some lines that should not be crossed.

All of this points to the urgent need for Christians to be involved not only in science but also in the ethics of science. Most of the essays in this section deal in one way or another with the moral questions that science raises and that only the Bible can answer.

27

EVOLUTION AS
RELIGION

*I*n the 1990s, the National Association of Biology Teachers (NABT) made a major change in its policy platform. The NABT is a professional society for college and high school teachers in the field of biology. It holds substantial influence over what is taught in American science classrooms.

The NABT Statement on Teaching Evolution used to include the following statement: "The diversity of life on Earth is the outcome of evolution: an unsupervised, impersonal, unpredictable and natural process." This policy had come under attack by, among others, prominent Christian philosopher Alvin Plantinga. Plantinga asked the NABT to remove the words *unsupervised* and *impersonal* from its creed. His point was that such language is unscientific. If life is unsupervised and impersonal, then it is not ruled by God. The NABT Statement on Teaching Evolution thus amounted to a defense of atheism. But that is a religious conviction, not a scientific one.

Initially the NABT was unwilling to make the change, but eventually they thought better of "taking a position on the religious question." The executive director admitted that their position "was interpreted to mean we were saying there is no God. We did not mean to imply that. That's beyond the purview of science."[1] The new NABT creed left open the possibility that a personal, intelligent Creator may have produced life through evolutionary mechanisms.

The policy change proved two things that critics of Darwinism have been saying for years. The first is that for many scientists, the evolutionary theory of the origin of life is a faith commitment. The idea that there has never been a God, only matter, has become a religion. Harvard genetics professor Richard Lewontin admitted as much in the *New York Review of Books*:

> We take the side of science *in spite of* the patent absurdity of some of its constructs, *in spite of* its failure to fulfill many of its extravagant promises of health and life, *in spite of* the tolerance of the scientific community for unsubstantiated just-so stories, because we have a prior commitment, a commitment to materialism.... Moreover, that materialism is absolute, for we cannot allow a Divine Foot in the door.[2]

One indication that the evolutionary account of origins has become a religion is the fact that some scientists argue that it is more than a theory. The late Carl Sagan went so far as to say, "The theory of evolution is as proved as is the fact that the earth goes around the sun." Sagan made this highly unscientific statement because every society needs a creation story to explain its existence. Charles Darwin wrote the modern creation story in 1859 (*The Origin of the Species*). It is a myth without a god. It says that life arose spontaneously and without purpose.

The other thing the change in the NABT policy suggests is that some evolutionists are less confident than they used to be. Indeed, there are some signs that the evolutionary account of the origin of life may be in trouble. Biochemist Michael Behe has shown that it is impossible for some complex cellular structures to evolve.[3] At the same time, many evolutionary theorists are engaged in bitter disputes about fundamental tenets of their theory.[4] Perhaps we are witnessing the beginning of the end of Darwinism.

Thinking Christians have always been open to whatever science has to teach about creation, including what it has to say about the diversity of life. God has revealed his glory in the book of nature as well as in the books of the Bible. What Christianity objects to is the godlessness of Darwinism, the way that it tries to turn the universe into a cosmic accident.

Although the Bible is not a science textbook, what it has to say about science is absolutely true and ought to be believed. So what does the Bible say about the origin of the world?

It insists, first of all, that God made everything there is: "In the beginning God created the heavens and the earth" (Gen. 1:1). The universe is not the product of blind chance. God made it all for his glory.

Second, the Bible allows for developmental changes to take place among the land creatures. God said, "Let the land produce living creatures according to their kinds: livestock, creatures that move along the ground, and wild animals, each according to its kind" (Gen. 1:24). By having the land produce the creatures, this verse implies that natural processes played some role in generating the diversity of the species.

However, this verse also makes it clear that God is responsible for the diversity of life on earth. As the Scripture goes on to say, "God made the wild animals according to their kinds, the livestock according to their kinds" (Gen. 1:25a). This is one place, incidentally, where the new NABT statement is misleading. It states that the "diversity of life on earth is the outcome of evolution." Yet the most important thing to be said is that the diversity of life comes from the creative activity of God, however he chose to do it.

A third thing the Bible teaches is the unique creation of Adam and Eve:

> Then God said, "Let us make man in our image, in our like-
> ness, and let them rule over the fish of the sea and the birds of the
> air, over the livestock, over all the earth, and over all the creatures
> that move along the ground."
>
> So God created man in his own image,
> in the image of God he created him;
> male and female he created them. (Gen. 1:26–27)

The religion of evolution denies the uniqueness of human beings. In the famous words of Cardinal Manning (1808–1892), if Darwinism is true, "There is no God and the ape is our Adam." However, the Bible insists that there is a God and that Adam was no ape. Human beings are not simply smarter than the average chimpanzee. We are a unique creation. In all the universe, we alone bear the divine image. And as the Bible goes on to explain in some detail, we alone bear moral responsibility for the fate of the universe.

These are a few of the things Genesis reveals about the creation of the world. The Bible does not reveal everything. And what it does not reveal is left open to scientific investigation, provided that scientists do not confuse their science with their religion.[5]

28

CELL DIVISION

*S*tem cells—the U.S. government has struggled to establish clear policies for this rapidly emerging area of scientific research.

Stem cells are generic cells that have the capacity to turn into any specific type of tissue. Stem cells specialize to become skin cells, muscle cells, nerve cells, or any of the more than two hundred other cell types in the human body. Their purpose is to repair or replace cells that have been damaged or destroyed. *Embryonic stem cells* are taken from fertilized eggs five or six days old. There are several ways to obtain them. One is to take them from fertility clinics, where thousands of unwanted embryos are stored in freezers, the product of in-vitro fertilization. Another is to extract clusters of cells from embryos made for the explicit purpose of medical research. Either way, the embryo is disassembled and destroyed in the process.

In 2001 the U.S. House of Representatives voted to ban the use of cloning to produce embryonic stem cells. In the words of Tom DeLay of Texas, "Human beings should not be cloned to stock a medical junkyard of spare parts for medical experimentation." But it was still up to President George Bush to decide whether or not the federal government should provide funding for research on stem cells obtained in other ways. Scientists in favor of such funding argue that this promising new area of medicine will combat degenerative diseases like Alzheimer's and ALS. Others say that manufacturing embryos in order to destroy them is simply murder in the name of medicine. In the end, the president cut the Gordian knot by allowing federally funded research (private research remains unaffected), but only on lines of stem cells already in existence. In theory this prevents any more embryos from being destroyed.

What is the biblical point of view? Is there a Christian ethic for stem cell research?

The Bible is consistently pro-life. Life is a gift from God, and therefore it is not to be destroyed carelessly. This is true for any form of life, but especially for life made in God's image. Human beings are stamped with the very likeness of God. This gives us a special dignity and demands our special protection.

The question is, When does human life begin? *Time* magazine's Michael Kinsley argues that the embryos used for stem cell research "are not fetuses with tiny, waving hands and feet. These are microscopic groupings of a few differentiated cells. There is nothing human about them."[1] But there is little doubt that an embryo *is* a human being. What else could it be? It must be human, because it is the genetic product of two other humans. It is also a living being—something capable of growing and developing . . . or dying. As the Ramsey Colloquium concluded in 1995, "Any being that is human is a human being."

Some ethicists quibble over the word "person." "Is an embryo really a *person*," they ask, "or does it merely have the potential to become a person?" Well, it all depends how one defines "person." Ethicists who think this way generally have difficulty explaining when a potential person becomes an actual person. What is certain is that an embryo is a human being. Indeed, it looks exactly like any other human being—including any one of us—at that stage of its development.

While no Bible verse states precisely when God puts his image in a person, the Bible clearly indicates that God's life-giving work goes back at least as far as conception. An important verse comes from David, who writes, "Surely I was sinful at birth, sinful from the time my mother conceived me" (Ps. 51:5). David was talking primarily about his sinful nature. First he said that he was sinful from birth, but then he realized that he was not going back far enough; he was a sinner from his very conception! There are other important verses as well. David said, "You created my inmost being; you knit me together in my mother's womb" (Ps. 139:13). Jeremiah dated God's claim on his life back before he was *in utero* (Jer. 1:5). Although these biblical writers were not familiar with the intricacies of stem cell research, they insisted on direct divine involvement from the very earliest stages of life.

Once we understand this, it becomes apparent why embryonic stem cell research is immoral: It inevitably involves the destruction of a human being designed to be in the image of God. In this respect, President Bush was right not to support the destruction of any additional embryos. However, the existing lines of stem cells—on which research will be permitted and funded—were themselves created by the same deadly process that the new policy denounces. This would seem to place future research done on them under a cloud of moral suspicion, not unlike the one that still surrounds data gathered from the Tuskegee study that allowed African-Americans to die from syphilis, or Mengele's experiments at Auschwitz. Furthermore, allowing even this limited use of stem cells inevitably opens the door for wider exploitation as more and more medical possibilities develop.

There is another reason why Christians should oppose embryonic stem cell research: It treats human beings as means to an end rather than as ends in themselves. Advocates of stem cell research invariably point out that such research may be useful in combating Parkinson's and other dreadful diseases. Even if this has not yet been proven, it is a worthy goal, and scientists should pursue any legitimate means to reduce human suffering. However, the worthiness of a goal does not set aside moral questions about how it is achieved. What is wrong to do is always wrong to do, even if it is done for the right reasons. To take a human embryo—which God has designed to be a person in its own right—and to use it for the purpose of medical research is to *misuse* it.

The question of means is especially relevant for stem cells because there is another way to get them. Stem cells can also be taken from living adults. Adult stem cells are not as versatile as embryonic stem cells (they cannot develop into every kind of cell, but only differentiate within the narrower limits of a cell type). However, the advantage is obvious: They can be collected without dehumanizing human beings by treating them like commodities, or even worse, killing them.

29

TAKE TWO PRAYERS
AND CALL ME IN THE
MORNING

*I*magine a medical treatment that would lower blood pressure, decrease the likelihood of catching a disease, speed recovery from surgery, improve chances of beating cancer, and generally increase a person's life span. It sounds almost too good to be true, especially if the treatment were known not to have any harmful side effects.

If there were such a treatment, it would be easy to market. People would buy it by the bottle, if not the case. It would make the cover of *Health* and *Reader's Digest*. Every doctor would recommend it.

Happily, such a precaution is readily available. A mounting body of medical research shows that regular church attendance, frequent prayer, and a personal relationship with God are among the strongest indicators of physical health. Religion is healthy. Knowing God does a body good.[1]

Here are some examples. A study from Dartmouth shows that the best predictor of surviving cardiac surgery is the strength of a patient's religious faith. The researchers were so impressed with the data that they wondered if doctors "may eventually be advised to make relatively simple inquiries about and reinforcement of . . . religious involvement as routinely as they inquire about cigarette smoking."

Other studies have focused on high blood pressure. In a survey of the research, Levin and Vanderpool show that men who feel religion is important and go to church every week have lower blood pressure than those who do not. In fact, even smokers who attend church are seven times less likely to have abnormally high blood pressure.

Still other scientific research shows that religious commitment decreases one's chances of drug abuse, protects against alcoholism, helps prevent depression, and lowers the rate of suicide.

What does all this data mean?

There are several things it does not mean. It does not mean that Christians never get sick or die. Obviously they do, because God's curse against sin affects us all. Born-again Christians are not immune to measles, cancer, AIDS, or any other disease. In the end, we all must die.

The other thing this data does not prove is the existence of God. It is evidence for God's existence, and it calls for an explanation. But it falls well short of a proof for God, especially if one is inclined to be a skeptic.

For one thing, showing a correlation between religion and good health does not prove causation, although it should be noted that the studies I mentioned controlled for related behaviors that might skew the results. Also, the research fails to discriminate between Christianity and other world religions. Finally, the only way any one ever comes to Christ is by the Holy Spirit speaking through Scripture, not by the latest scientific finding.

Yet the body of research on religion and health is significant. It shows that human beings are made to worship God. God has made us to know him with our whole person. He made our bodies to rest and worship one full day in seven. He made our souls to find peace through prayer. We omit these spiritual duties at our peril. Not worshiping God is self-destructive, physically as well as spiritually.

The link between health and religion is also a reminder that God answers prayer. A famous study by Randolph Byrd examined the effect of intercessory prayer on coronary patients. Patients were divided into two groups—one to be prayed for and the other not. Then committed Christians were solicited to pray every day for half of the patients. None of the doctors, nurses, or patients knew who was in which group. Yet the ones who were prayed for had significantly lower incidence of heart failure, cardiopulmonary arrest, and infection.

Given the way God loves to answer prayer, this was to be expected. "Is any one of you sick?" writes the apostle James. "He should call the elders of the church to pray over him and anoint him with oil in the name of the Lord" (James 5:14). This is not a medicinal remedy, as some have suggested, but a spiritual one. What is important is not so much the oil as the prayer of faith. God answers prayers for healing, as some research shows.

It would be good for Christians in medicine to become familiar with these medical studies. There is now scientific evidence that prayer and church attendance lead to longer, healthier lives. In fact, infrequent church attendance is a risk factor for disease. It is not healthy not to go to church!

This gives Christian doctors and nurses some medical reasons to raise spiritual questions with their patients. Medical colleagues should be alerted that religion plays an important role in health. It is in the medical interests of patients to attend church, to pray, and to have a relationship with God.

Obviously these issues need to be raised with sensitivity. Some patients may not want to talk about God (although three out of four Americans feel their physician should address spiritual issues as a regular part of medical care). In some cases, it may be appropriate to ask if a patient prays or attends church and then to mention that this is known to be good for one's health.

However doctors and nurses are able to use this medical information, it is good to be reminded of what we already know: it is good to know and to worship God. It is good for the body as well as the soul.

30

HOMO SAPIENS
FOR SALE

$\mathcal{M}$any observers are starting to call the twenty-first century "the biotech century." Recent advances in biology and technology suggest that in the next one hundred years human beings will have unprecedented opportunities to create, manipulate, and destroy themselves.

Consider a few examples. Within the next few years scientists will perfect their map of the human genetic code. The Human Genome Project, as it is called, reproduces the complete sequence of the three billion chemical pairs that make up human DNA.

This genetic information has a number of potential uses and abuses. It raises the possibility of what biotech critic Jeremy Rifkin calls "the ultimate shopping experience": designer babies, or children whose DNA is altered to produce specific physical or intellectual traits. Also, doctors are beginning to practice gene therapy, adding good genes to the cells of sick patients in order to make them better. Then there is genetic enhancement, in which genes are altered to prevent disease or extend the human life span.

Significant research is also being done on human stem cells, which are cells that have not yet differentiated into blood, bone, brain, or other kinds of cells. Stem cells have the capacity to become any part of the human body, raising the possibility that one day scientists will be able to start growing human organs in a petri dish.

There are other developments as well. More discussions and possibly more experiments are taking place on the cloning of human beings. Perhaps by the end of the next century, biochemists will complete a map of the more than ten billion neurons in the human brain, thus closing the gap between real and artificial intelligence.

All of this research confirms two fundamental aspects of human nature: creativity and depravity. The fact that we are able to radically change our bodies shows that we are creators made in the image of a creative God. The fact that we do it without stopping to think about the moral implications of what we are doing shows that we are base sinners.

Scientists are no more depraved than anyone else, although some of them seem to have an unjustified belief in their divinity. Some scientists believe that we must do anything we can do. Yet the truth is that there are lots of things we can do but mustn't. For the foreseeable future, Christians will have to wrestle constantly with the ethical and theological implications of new biotechnology.

One fundamental principle can help us evaluate what we should and should not be doing. The principle is: *Don't use people.* Treat human beings as ends rather than as means to an end.

The reason we should not use people has to do with who we are, which is where our culture has lost its way. We are rapidly losing track of true human identity. In the words of one observer, "We don't know what to make of ourselves precisely because we are, more than ever, able to re-make ourselves."[1]

If we want to know what human beings are really for, we have to go back to the Bible. There we discover that we are made in "the image and glory of God" (1 Cor. 11:7). A human being is a male or a female made in God's image and created for God's glory.

There are plenty of things, therefore, that a human being is not. A human being is not a repository of spare body parts. A human being is not a bag of chemicals or a network of neurons. A human being is not what one professor calls "a machine made out of meat."[2] Nor is a human being a commodity whose genes can be harvested as the ultimate human resource. A human being is a person made to glorify God and enjoy him forever.

When we remember how God made human beings in the first place (according to the pattern of his image) and why he made them (for his glory), we start to get answers to some of our questions about biotechnology. If human beings are creatures made in God's image, there are plenty of things we can rule out.

We can rule out the preposterous idea of patenting the human genome. Many scientific researchers are rushing to claim parts of the human genetic code. This is without precedent. The U.S. Patent Office has never before awarded a patent for what is known as a "discovery of nature." In other words, scientists have never been allowed to claim credit for God's handiwork. To do so with the human genome is to treat a person almost like a human invention.

We can also rule out any form of genetic research that ends up discarding human embryos. This is obviously to treat a person—for what is a human embryo if not a human being?—as a means rather than as an end. For the same reason, we can rule out any form of scientific work that requires the use of aborted fetal tissue, as most stem-cell research does.

There are a host of ethical problems with human cloning. One reason the quest to clone human beings should be abandoned is that every conceivable clone would be made, not in the interests of the clone, but in the interests of whoever wants the clone made. In other words, cloning treats human beings as means to an end rather than as ends in themselves.

Much more could be said about the biotech century, but this is a good place to start: a human being is a creature made in God's image. So don't use people.

31

EARTH DAY

*S*everal years ago a group of French farmers staged a protest against the European Union. In the middle of the night they transplanted a wheat field onto the most famous boulevard in Paris, the Champs Elysées. The field came complete with cows and sheep. When Parisians awoke the next morning, rather than getting angry, they began to frolic in the field. Whatever else the protest may have accomplished, it succeeded in reminding the city that humanity's first habitat was a garden.

Earth Day is a day to remember that our responsibility to care for our planet goes all the way back to Adam and Eve in the garden of Eden. Yet I wonder how many Christians mark the occasion in any significant way. Although caring for the environment is high on the secular agenda, it does not get much attention in the evangelical church. In fact, many Christians get suspicious when politicians start talking about the environment.

There are some good reasons for this. The way we respond to the universe always says something about our ultimate religious commitment, and many approaches to the environment are hostile to biblical Christianity. Evolutionists minimize the unique status of human beings as creatures made in the image of God. The New Age movement honors the earth as our mother. Similarly, the Gaia Hypothesis treats our planet like a female deity. The problem with these worldviews is that they mistake the creation for the Creator. Rather than trying to protect the earth, they bow down and worship it.

Given all this neo-paganism, it is not surprising that most Christians have little in common with people for whom environmentalism is a way of life. Nevertheless environmentalists have the right impulse: They recognize that the world is precious and that human beings have a responsibility to preserve it. The noted evolutionary biologist E. O. Wilson argues that we must "see humanity as part of the biosphere and its faithful steward, not just the resident master and economic maximizer."[1] That is a surprisingly Christian approach to the environment. It places our life on this planet under the category of stewardship. We are part of the biosphere; thus we share something in common with every other creature. But there is also something special about us, something that requires us not to use the planet but to care for it.

Without getting into scientific disputes over global warming or the depletion of the ozone layer, it is safe to say that the earth is in more urgent need of care now than at any time since the days of Noah. In the summer of 2000 the United Nations released its analysis of global ecosystems. The study was the most sweeping report of its kind, analyzing the stability of the world's coastal, agricultural, fresh water, grassland, and forest ecosystems. Needless to say, the news was not encouraging. By any objective measure, human beings are doing unprecedented damage to the earth.

This calls for theological comment. The first thing to recognize is that the earth is our home—not our permanent home, but our home nonethe-less. God has settled us on this good earth. As Paul said to the people of Lystra, "He has shown kindness by giving you rain from heaven and crops in their seasons; he provides you with plenty of food and fills your hearts with joy" (Acts 14:17).

When God planted us on earth, he told us to make ourselves at home. We have divine permission to make use of every animal and every plant. God said to Adam and Eve, "Fill the earth and subdue it. Rule over the fish of the sea and the birds of the air and over every living creature that moves on the ground. . . . I give you every seed-bearing plant on the face of the whole earth and every tree that has fruit with seed in it" (Gen. 1:28b-29a). Theologians call this the "creation mandate." It means that human beings have the right to use (but not "use up") all of the world's resources.

With that right goes the weighty responsibility to cherish what God has made: "The LORD God took the man and put him in the Garden of Eden to work it and take care of it" (Gen. 2:15). We are called to be earth keepers, and thus we answer to God for every use and abuse of the world that he has made.

The problem is that our world is spoiled by sin. Think of the defor-estation of the Amazon and the destruction of cod fisheries in the North Atlantic. Lament the plight of battery hens that are forced to lay eggs day and night, or the loss of countless species through pollution. Surely these examples of greed and negligence are part of what the Bible means when it describes the "whole creation . . . groaning as in the pains of childbirth" (Rom. 8:22). Creation suffers the sad consequences of human sin.

If sin is the problem, then ultimately salvation is the answer. The whole universe shares a common destiny with us, for the plan of redemp-tion is cosmic in its scope. To challenge the popular slogan, there is no need for us to "save Planet Earth" because God will save the world in his good time. The day will come when "the creation itself will be liberated from its bondage to decay and brought into the glorious freedom of the children of God" (Rom. 8:21).

In the meantime, we are commanded to be faithful stewards of the world and everything in it. Keep America beautiful. Help plants and animals grow and flourish. Do not squander food, water, or energy. Do this not because we are running out of natural resources or because it is unfair for us to use more than our share, but because everything God has made is precious. To be wasteful is to be disrespectful to our Creator. Wherever we go, we are to remember that this is our Father's world and that he has called us to care for it.

One family I know celebrated Earth Day 2000 by participating in the community cleanup of a stream near their house. As they joined their neighbors in picking up trash and clearing away debris, they were doing something that was not only environmentally sound but also spiritually sound. Taking care of the earth is good, practical, biblical Christianity.

32

DIGITAL ANGEL

*W*henever God does something really big, it usually involves angels. This was true at the first Christmas, when a company of the heavenly host appeared to shepherds announcing good news of great joy.

It was also true at the first Easter. The women who went to the garden met angels at the empty tomb. The Gospel of Matthew describes an angel whose "appearance was like lightning," and whose "clothes were white as snow" (Matt. 28:3). Similarly, the Gospel of Luke describes the sudden appearance of "two men in clothes that gleamed like lightning" (Luke 24:4). The angels were there to herald the resurrection of Jesus Christ and to give messages of guidance and comfort. Their presence was a sign of salvation, for whenever God decides to say it with angels, he must be doing something *really* important.

The word *angel* means "messenger," and angels are God's messengers. By all accounts, they are terrifying to meet. Apparently angels know this, because in the Bible the first thing they almost always say is what the angel said to the women at the empty tomb: "Do not be afraid." Angels are dazzling, adorned with a bright and shining majesty. There is nothing else like them.

That being the case, a product introduced by Applied Digital Solutions (ADS) seems almost blasphemous. Not long ago, at an invitation-only event in New York City, ADS unveiled the future of electronic surveillance. The new technology is a "miniature digital transceiver"—a tiny microchip implanted under the skin, which can monitor vital signs and track a human being anywhere on planet earth. ADS promotes the new device—commonly referred to as the Digital Angel—as the ultimate solution for finding kidnapped children, locating lost skiers, tracking prisoners of war, and rescuing elderly persons who have fallen and can't get up.[1]

In its patent application, ADS described its invention as "the world's first digital tracking device," a technology "unlike anything ever created." What makes the device unique is its power supply, which is generated electromechanically through the wearer's muscle movement.

Since the product is still under development, it is too early to tell how the Digital Angel will be used. One possible use is firearms safety: a weapon could be developed that would fire only if a chip in the gun matched a chip implanted in the gun's owner. However, many other potential uses are more sinister. One can imagine a government requiring newborns to be given digital angels as a safety precaution or as an aid to law enforcement. One can also imagine vendors using personal microchips to locate potential customers or financial institutions requiring them as a way of verifying each and every transaction.

In the hands of a totalitarian government, this wireless guardian would be an unprecedented mechanism for social control and the invasion of personal privacy. Some Christians will no doubt think of the beast in Revelation, who "forced everyone, small and great, rich and poor, free and slave, to receive a mark on his right hand or on his forehead, so that no one could buy or sell unless he had the mark" (Rev. 13:16–17a).

ADS has no intention of becoming a tool for the Antichrist. The company's stated intentions are benevolent. In the words of head scientist Peter Zhou, the Digital Angel will function as "a connection from yourself to the electronic world. It will be your guardian, protector . . . a hybrid of electronic intelligence and your own soul." Personally, I'm not sure I want to be so closely connected to the electronic world. But even apart from the inevitably dehumanizing effect of becoming digitized, it is doubtful whether a Digital Angel is an improvement over the real thing.

The Bible teaches that angels are charged with the responsibility of watching over God's people. Consider the following Bible verses: "The angel of the LORD encamps around those who fear him, and he delivers them" (Ps. 34:7); "See that you do not look down on one of these little ones. For I tell you that their angels in heaven always see the face of my Father in heaven" (Matt. 18:10). Other verses show that angels keep an eye on what is happening in the church (1 Cor. 11:10) and watch over believers at the time of death (Luke 16:22). On occasion, they are called to rescue us from danger (see Dan. 3:28; 6:22; Acts 5:19–20; 12:7–11). In short, angels take care of God's people from birth to death, at home and away from home. As the psalmist says, "He will command his angels concerning you to guard you in all your ways" (Ps. 91:11).

Now that's what I call a guardian angel! Although we are almost never aware of their presence, angels are always on the job—surrounding, delivering, protecting, helping, watching, keeping, and guarding. The Bible thus calls angels "ministering spirits sent to serve those who will inherit salvation" (Heb. 1:14).

The ministry of angels is a sign of the special divine favor that rests upon God's people. Earlier I mentioned that whenever God does something really big, it usually involves angels. By that reasoning, the life of every individual Christian must be of some importance. Apparently our service is of sufficient value to God that he offers us the assistance of angels.

Guardian angels will carry on their ministry of protection and preservation right up until the next big event in the history of salvation: the return of Christ in all his glory. Angels will be involved then too, for according to Scripture, "[God] will send his angels with a loud trumpet call, and they will gather his elect from the four winds, from one end of the heavens to the other" (Matt. 24:31). No doubt we will be amazed at the sight of these angels. But they will not be surprised to see us, for they are watching over us all the time.

PART 6

SOCIAL ISSUES

Surely if men were careful to reform themselves first, and then their own families, they should see God's manifold blessings in our land and upon church and commonwealth. For of particular persons come families; of families, towns; of towns, provinces; of provinces, whole realms.

—RICHARD GREENHAM

The contemporary church does not seem to occupy very much cultural territory. The news media have become almost entirely secular. The major colleges and universities have long since abandoned their Christian heritage. There are few Christians of note in entertainment and the arts, and many professionals in these fields actively oppose the gospel. Some Christians still try to flex their political muscle, but even here the evangelical influence seems to be getting weaker.

In places where Christians actually do engage with culture, they tend to erect separate institutions. We have our own newsmagazines, our own colleges, and our own artists and entertainers, but they seem to live in some parallel universe. And as far as culture is concerned, this universe rarely has much influence on the one that everyone else inhabits.

Almost the only area where Christians are still vocal is public ethics. On issues like homosexuality, abortion, and school choice, the evangelical viewpoint is widely known, even if it is still largely discounted. One reason for this discount is that evangelical opinions on social issues tend to be shrill. What is needed instead is an articulate, carefully reasoned, and yet passionate presentation of the biblical point of view on the full range of social problems.

Many of the essays in this section of *My Father's World* deal with social issues that are high on the evangelical agenda: abortion, infanticide, pornography, drug abuse, and gambling. Others deal with issues that are less closely tied to the church but where Christian theology has something important to say: human rights, cheating, sports, and the righteous use of the automobile.

It is often said that a good Christian should have the Bible in one hand and a newspaper in the other. This statement acknowledges that as Christians we should be concerned about the world and its problems. On the one hand, we have the latest news about what is happening in our Father's world. On the other hand, we have the revelation of our Father's Word, the ultimate source of authority for all of life's problems. All we need to do is keep a firm grip on the Bible and the newspaper.

There are several problems with this analogy. One is the difficulty of reading two things at once, to say nothing of the near impossibility of reading a newspaper with only one hand! But our real problem is in knowing how the Bible relates to what we are reading in the newspaper. Many Christians listen to the news, and many still read their Bibles, but how many can use their biblical knowledge to analyze current events from the Christian point of view? The following essays may help to show how this can be done.

33

WHY HUMANS HAVE RIGHTS

*P*eople do not ask for their rights any more, they demand them. They seek liberty without responsibility. They say, "Hey, I've got my rights!" And all too often, when people start insisting on their rights, they are really asking for new and special privileges.

This is not the way human rights were understood when the United Nations approved its Universal Declaration of Human Rights in 1948. That declaration is worth pondering because it is the most important statement from the twentieth century about what human beings are and what they are for.

The Bible does not speak about human rights, at least in so many words. It hardly ever talks about what other people owe us. It is much more concerned with what we owe to others—things like acting justly and loving mercy (Mic. 6:8). Nevertheless many parts of the Universal Declaration of Human Rights reflect biblical truth. The document stands as a monument to God's common grace. It is also a monument to God's saving grace, because some of the men who wrote it—men like Charles Malik (1906–1987) and Jacques Maritain(1882–1973)—wrote from the standpoint of the Christian worldview.

The Declaration's preamble affirms "the dignity and worth of the human person." There is something unique about every human being, something to be prized and protected. The document then tries to explain why this is true. It is because human beings are "endowed with reason and conscience" and are able to "act towards one another in a spirit of brotherhood" (Article 1).

This is true enough, but it does not quite explain the reason human beings are so valuable. It is because we are created in the "image and likeness of God" (Gen. 1:26–27). The one who has endowed us with reason and conscience is our Creator. But at least the document recognizes that there is something special about human beings. We all deserve respect: "Everyone is entitled to all the rights and freedoms set forth in this Declaration, without distinction of any kind, such as race, color, sex, language, religion, political or other opinion, national or social origin, property, birth, or other status" (Article 2).

In keeping with biblical teaching, the UN declaration takes its stand against injustices such as slavery, torture, and false arrest. It preserves the freedom of religion, including the freedom to change religions: "Everyone has the right to freedom of thought, conscience, and religion; this right includes freedom to change his religion or belief, and freedom, either alone or in community with others and in public or private, to manifest his religion or belief in teaching, practice, worship, and observance" (Article 18). This is an important article because many Communist and Islamic countries deny citizens the right to convert to Christianity.

The U.N. Declaration shows respect for the family as well as the individual. It offers special protections for mothers and children. It identifies the family as the "natural and fundamental group unit of society" (Article 16). This too is part of God's plan, that human society should be founded upon stable families.

Then there are the comments the declaration makes about work and leisure. Here too the view is roughly biblical. Everyone should work, and in just and favorable conditions (Article 23). Everyone "has the right to rest and leisure" (Article 24). This, of course, is the reason for the biblical Sabbath. God has made us in such a way that we flourish when we maintain regular rhythms of work and rest.

Perhaps the most surprising thing about the Universal Declaration of Human Rights is that it understands that rights are really responsibilities. These days a right has come to mean something that everyone else owes me. But that is not how the UN declaration understands a right. Article 29 clearly explains that everyone "has duties to the community" and that the purpose of the law is to show "respect for the rights and freedoms of others."

Properly understood, a human right is not something I insist on for myself; it is a responsibility I undertake for someone else. This is close to the biblical view of love: treating my neighbor as myself (Matt. 22:39). As the Scripture says, "Each of you should look not only to your own interests, but also to the interests of others" (Phil. 2:4).

All of these principles fit in well with a biblical view of the world. If these are what human rights are, then Christianity is all for them: the dignity of humanity, the cry for justice, the freedom to worship, the sanctity of the family, and the balance between work and leisure.

There is only one major problem with the Universal Declaration of Human Rights: human beings. The declaration was written while the wounds of the Second World War were still fresh. It was a response to the horrific events of the 1940s, especially the Holocaust in Nazi Germany. It was written because "disregard and contempt for human rights have resulted in barbarous acts which have outraged the conscience of mankind" (Preamble).

Unfortunately, not much has changed since 1948. Disregard and contempt for human life continue to result in barbarous acts that outrage the human conscience. The UN declaration has been unable to stop the atrocities that have occurred since the end of World War II. It could not stop the gulags of the Soviet Union, the ethnic cleansing in the Balkans, or the wanton slaughter carried out by dictators like Pol Pot and Idi Amin. It has never been able to deliver what it promised: "a social and international order in which rights and freedoms" are "fully realized." In that respect, at least, the Universal Declaration of Human Rights has been a universal failure.

UN Secretary-General Kofi Annan described the 1948 declaration as "the highest of human aspirations." If that is true, then the best humanity has to offer is not good enough. It is not good enough to bring peace on earth and good will to men. Only God can do that, and only through his Prince of Peace (Isa. 9:6). Yet Jesus Christ is conspicuous by his absence from the UN declaration. When the document was first written, Jacques Maritain said, "Yes, we agree about the rights, but on condition no one asks us why." Why do human beings have rights? As long as that question remains unanswered, human beings will not be treated with the respect they deserve.

34

ASHKELON IN AMERICA

*A*shkelon was never known for its godliness. It was one of the five major cities in Philistia, and it seems always to have been a wicked place. Most of the references to Ashkelon in the Bible are prophecies of judgment. The Philistines were enemies of God. They often attacked his people, as they did in the days of Goliath. Thus Jeremiah promised that Ashkelon would be silenced (Jer. 47:5), Zephaniah prophesied that the city would be left in ruins (Zeph. 2:4), and Zechariah said it would be deserted (Zech. 9:5).

Archaeologists recently found something horrific in Ashkelon.[1] There is a building there that clearly can be identified as a bathhouse, apparently built some centuries after the biblical prophets. It contains a tub and a hypocaust, an underfloor furnace used to heat water. What archaeologists wondered was whether the bathhouse also served as a brothel. Mixed bathing often led to sexual immorality in those days. Besides, the inscription on the side of the bathing area was suggestive. It read "Enter, enjoy and . . ."

Then came a startling discovery. The alley behind the bathhouse contained a sewer filled with rubbish. In the rubbish there were nearly one hundred tiny skeletons, all discarded within a day or two of birth. Closer examination revealed that the infants had been drowned.

Then came a further discovery. DNA testing revealed that nearly all the infants who had been exposed were males. This was a major surprise. Infanticide was an accepted practice in many ancient cultures, but only for girls. Although they were sometimes considered expendable, no one ever got rid of their baby boys. In a letter dating from the time of Christ, one man wrote to his wife, "I ask and beg you to take good care of our baby son. . . . If you are delivered of child [before I get home], if it is a boy keep it; if a girl, discard it."[2]

Why, then, were so many boys left out in the alley in Ashkelon? The most likely explanation is that the bathhouse doubled as a bordello. Boys would not be kept, but girls could grow up to learn the trade. What the archaeologists found, therefore, was a scene of unspeakable squalor: a back-alley brothel where courtesans dumped human beings in the sewer.

But then there really is no pretty way to get rid of newborns. Our country too has places of unspeakable squalor, such as the dumpster behind the abortion clinic, to name one.

Every January on Sanctity of Life Sunday Christians pause to lament the deadly and barbaric evil of abortion. There is little new to say on the subject each year because little has changed since Roe vs. Wade. Americans still defend a woman's right to kill. And this means that little has changed in the last two thousand years. We are still Philistines.

In America, as in Ashkelon, there are people who believe it is okay to kill as long you stay in business. This is why abortion is so common in our country. The abortion rate has started to decline, but only slightly. In Pennsylvania abortions are down by 2 percent. However, nationwide nearly a million and a half abortions are still performed every year.

Another thing that has not changed is that abortion is still wrong. Not long ago Greg Koukl observed, "If the unborn is not a person, no justification for abortion is necessary. However, if the unborn is a person, no justification for abortion is adequate."[3] And an unborn child *is* a person. We know this because the Bible teaches that God's work in a person's life begins in the womb, if not earlier. A fetus is a person, made in the image and likeness of God, living in relationship to other persons. Therefore, to take the life of a fetus is to take the life of a human person.

Another thing that has not changed is that we are still a long way away from eliminating abortion in America. Efforts to legislate morality are proving to be as ineffective as efforts to protest against immorality. Out of frustration, some Christians now advocate the use of violence to stop doctors from performing abortions. But that is not the biblical answer, either. God considers our hatred as sinful as someone else's murder (Matt. 5:21–22). His way is the way of the cross, not the sword.

We must recognize that there are some wrongs we cannot right. God does not enable us to make a just society in our strength or in our time. There are times when the church seems powerless in the face of social evil. But even wrongs that cannot be righted can be lamented.

A culture that refuses to weep over its sins will eventually cry out in the pains of judgment. Some day God will judge America the way he judged Ashkelon. Those who take life will have life taken from them. But the people of God will cry long before that day comes. We will shed tears for the unwanted pregnancies and the unwelcomed children. We will mourn the terminated pregnancies and the partial-birth abortions. We will weep with the mothers—and the fathers—who later have remorse for what they have done. We will lament all the wrongs we cannot make right. And we will wait for God, somehow, to make things right in the end.

35

THE MASSACRE OF THE INNOCENTS

*M*y three-year old son was the first to notice them, lying in a jumble at the bottom of the page. "What are those from, Mommy?"

What should a mother say to her toddler when he is surprised by sin? What should she say when the jumble at the bottom of the page is a pile of corpses?

Lisa and Josh had been reading the Christmas story—the story of the Son of God coming into the world, paraphrased by Madeleine L'Engle. The pictures were full color reproductions of Giotto's (c. 1266–1337) paintings of the life of Christ from the Scrovegni Chapel in Padua. Mother and child had come to the painting entitled "The Massacre of the Innocents," which depicts King Herod's soldiers searching for the baby Jesus and putting the infants of Judea to the sword.[1] The results of their grisly labors lie underfoot, naked at the bottom of the page. What should a mother say?

At least Herod's soldiers did not drive their swords through the hearts of their own children. A mother might just be able to explain a man hating another man's child. But how could she possibly explain to her child that some mommies and daddies don't love their own babies? How could she possibly explain the damnable doctrine of abortion, that somebody else has to die because I want to be happy?

The fact is that there are a lot of corpses lying in a jumble at the bottom of American society. State laws restricting late-term abortions have been declared unconstitutional. Late-term abortions, which were once banned but are now deemed constitutionally protected, are too gruesome to describe. We must avert our gaze, just as we avert our gaze from Giotto's "Massacre of the Innocents." And yet federal courts have declared not simply that this ghastly procedure may be allowed but that it must be allowed if America's constitutional democracy is to remain intact. In order for our society to remain standing, they have said, we must stand on top of the corpses of little children.

That is why it is good for us, on the third Sunday of every January, to remember the massacre of the innocents. On Sanctity of Life Sundays it is important to say something about the biblical teaching on abortion, to be reminded that one proper response to abortion is abhorrence.

"You shall not murder" (Ex. 20:13). This fundamental protection for the sanctity of human life comes from the Ten Commandments. It is part of God's charter for human conduct. Why shouldn't we murder? Because men, women, and children are made in the image of God. "So God created man in his own image," the Scripture says, "in the image of God he created him; male and female he created them" (Gen. 1:27). Men and women and children are like coins that bear the impression of a nation's sovereign. To deface such a coin is an affront to the ruler who is represented on its face. Similarly, murder is an offense against both humanity and the God who made humanity.

But what about abortion? Does abortion count as murder? Is the sanctity of human life violated when a doctor removes a fetus from a womb? Does a fetus bear the image of God, or does this status apply only to children who have drawn their first breath?

Many things can be said about the uniqueness of the human being that is formed when sperm and egg unite, about the life and vitality of the fetus in the womb. And many things can be said about the child's mental capacities, response to pain, and experience of relationship with father and mother prior to birth. To watch the ultrasound of a fetus is to gain a thousand proofs of the child's humanity.

But even apart from all these things, it is enough to know that a child is created by God from the moment of conception. The lordship of Jesus Christ over the human being does not begin at birth but extends back into the womb. This is what David had to say about God's work within his mother's body:

> For you created my inmost being;
>> you knit me together in my mother's womb.
> I praise you because I am fearfully and wonderfully made;
>> your works are wonderful,
>> I know that full well.
> My frame was not hidden from you
>> when I was made in the secret place.
> When I was woven together in the depths of the earth,
>> your eyes saw my unformed body. (Ps. 139:13–16a)

These verses speak of the intimate relationship between God and the unborn child. God's creative act begins at conception, with the formation of the child's inmost being and the fashioning of the child's frame. What the psalmist says about the unformed body exposes the evil of abortion. A woman and her doctor may hide an unborn child from the world, but the child is not hidden from God. Even an embryo is a fearful and wonderful work of God, knit and woven together by his Almighty hand. Even before a fetus can be recognized as a human being visibly, the child is known by God in a personal way. And that is what it means to be a person, to be a human being to whom God relates in a personal way.

The Bible teaches that abortion is a sin. But it does more than condemn sin; it also offers forgiveness. I wish my son had not discovered those babies lying in a jumble at the bottom of the page. More than that, I wish that page were not in the book. The book holds a certain horror for me now, the horror of the violence committed and the dark secret uncovered. Even more than that, I wish that King Herod had never tried to kill Jesus Christ, so that there had never been a need for Giotto to paint "The Massacre of the Innocents." But there was a need. The massacre did occur, and to ignore the infants at the bottom of the page would be to trample them all over again.

Giotto needed to paint those infants because he needed to present humanity as it is, in all of its sinfulness and barbarity. For it was this humanity that Jesus Christ embraced in his incarnation. Jesus entered the human race just because of its sinfulness and barbarity. He came in the flesh to bring sinners to justice—and to make atonement for sin.

On the walls of the Scrovegni Chapel there is another painting of still greater horror. It is a painting of Jesus Christ, dying on a cross to pay "for the sins of the whole world" (1 John 2:2). Giotto needed to paint that picture because it too belongs on the pages of our story.

What the crucified Christ offers is forgiveness for sins, even the most abhorrent of sins, such as infanticide and abortion. There is a soldier in Giotto's "Crucifixion," holding a spear and gazing at Christ on the cross. I sometimes wonder if he might have been one of Herod's soldiers. If so, and if at the cross he repented of his sins and trusted in Jesus for forgiveness, then his evil part in "The Massacre of the Innocents" would have been forgiven. For the sacrifice of Christ is sufficient for any sinner who repents. It is sufficient for the abortionist. It is sufficient for the woman who has killed her own unborn child. It is sufficient for me, and for you.

36

THE LUST OF
THE EYES

*H*uman beings—especially men—have always struggled with lust, in the sexual sense of the word. Job was the holiest of the ancients, yet even he had to make "a covenant with [his] eyes not to look lustfully at a girl" (Job 31:1). The apostle John warned against "the cravings of sinful man, the lust of his eyes" (1 John 2:16). In the third century, the theologian Origen (c. 185–254) was so distressed by his sexual sin that he crushed his testicles between two bricks. Or consider America's greatest theologian—Jonathan Edwards (1703–1758)—who lamented the prevalence of gross sexual immorality in (of all places) Puritan New England. Like any other sin, the lust of the eyes has always been with us.

What is new, however, is the unprecedented access we have to sexual images. There are pornographic magazines and videos. There are adult bookstores and strip clubs. There are pornographic programs on cable television, and perhaps most alarmingly of all, there are thousands of ways to access pornography over the Internet. A study by psychologists at Stanford and Duquesne universities reports that some twenty million Americans visit sexual Web sites each month, of whom perhaps two hundred thousand are addicted to cybersex.[1] How many of them, one wonders, are members of a Bible-teaching church?

Using pornography is a sin, which is why people view it in secret and why they feel ashamed when they do. Because it is a hidden sin, its destructive power is immense. Lust is never satisfied; it always craves more. Thus pornography is uncontrollable. What at first is only idle curiosity soon becomes an addiction and may ultimately lead to more vulgar sins such as prostitution. Along the way, pornography kills joy and inhibits intimacy. Often it hinders a single person from finding a life partner. Frequently it rips a marriage from seam to seam. Always it disturbs a man's communion with God, robbing his confidence in the power of the gospel to bring spiritual change. It may even destroy his soul.

The masturbation that often accompanies the viewing of pornographic images is also a sin. I mention this because people sometimes claim that masturbation is not forbidden in the Bible. It is true that masturbation is never explicitly mentioned. Neither is pornography, for that matter, or many other specific kinds of sexual sin. Instead, the Bible is content to address sexual sin in general terms, outlawing any sexual activity outside the union of husband and wife. Paul exhorted the Ephesians: "But among you there must not be even a hint of sexual immorality, or of any kind of impurity . . . because these are improper for God's holy people" (Eph. 5:3). Sex is for sharing. By turning sexual gratification back upon the self, masturbation is perhaps the most intense form of self-worship imaginable.

Christians who are in bondage to sexual sin often hope to find a quick fix for their addiction. There are no quick fixes. If there were, someone would have discovered one by now. The reason no one has is because sexual sin goes down to the deepest levels of the sinful nature.

Even if there are no quick fixes, there are some things that people in the grip of sexual sin can do. The first is to admit one's desperate need of spiritual help. Confess sexual addiction, not only to God, who alone can forgive sin, but also to a mature Christian: "Confess your sins to each other and pray for each other so that you may be healed" (James 5:16). Anyone who fights against lust needs some allies. Do not be deceived: This is not a problem Christians can conquer on their own, in isolation from other Christians. More than almost any other kind of sin, sexual immorality thrives on secrecy. But as soon as the secret is out, sexual sin starts to loosen its hold on the body and the soul: "He who conceals his sins does not prosper, but whoever confesses and renounces them finds mercy" (Prov. 28:13). Anyone struggling with sexual sin should make a commitment to talk with a Christian brother or sister as soon as possible.

The second thing to do is limit access to pornographic images. Instead of hoarding lewd magazines or pictures, go home and throw them away. If pornographic movies are a stumbling block, terminate the cable package and stop driving by the adult bookstore. Cancel credit cards; end the Internet account; stay out of the gay bar; ask the hotel to remove the TV—do whatever it takes to radically reduce temptation to sin.

By itself, however, getting rid of pornographic images is not enough. The real problem is not on the computer screen, it is in the heart, which is why trying to "just say no" never works. If it were simply a matter of physical pleasure, sexual sin could be conquered through self-discipline, the exertion of moral effort. But sex is always a spiritual matter, and gaining victory over sexual sin requires a deep and gracious work of God's Spirit.

Understand that giving in to pornography and lust reflects an inability to give and to receive love. It is an attempt to escape from a world that seems unresponsive to our desire for acceptance and significance. The escape is only an illusion; the relief is only temporary, and it always leads to even deeper disappointment and despair. Dr. Harry W. Schaumburg writes, "Sexual addiction is the by-product of intense unmet needs, coupled with the demand for fulfillment and control of relational pain independently of God. . . . Sexual addiction isn't just an issue of sex or even external behavior: it's a by-product of loneliness, pain, the self-centered demand to be loved and accepted regardless of the consequences, and a loss of vital relationship with God."[2]

The fact that sexual sin is about something more than sex has a number of significant implications. It means that conquering sexual addiction requires the fresh application of repentance and forgiveness to the deepest wounds of the heart. It also means that there are many other sins that need to be dealt with—sins like arrogance, bitterness, and self-deception—before anyone can make significant progress toward holiness. In some cases, it also means coming to terms with the ways that we have been sinned against, especially if we have suffered sexual abuse.

The ultimate antidote to lust is love—real love—the kind of selfless love that Christ demonstrated on the cross. And love is one thing that God has in unlimited supply. He alone has the love to forgive our darkest sins, to satisfy our deepest desires, and to replace our lust with joy: "At one time we too were foolish, disobedient, deceived and enslaved by all kinds of passions and pleasures. . . . But when the kindness and love of God our Savior appeared, he saved us" (Titus 3:3–4).

37

ALCOHOL LICENSE

From time to time, Tenth Presbyterian Church is asked to approve the alcohol license for a nearby restaurant. There is a civic ordinance that requires businesses within so many feet of a church to obtain consent before they are granted a license to sell drinks. Depending on the nature of the establishment (we said no to a gay strip club), we are usually happy to comply.

We are also happy to allow church members to consume alcohol. This is because the Bible teaches that Christians have the liberty to drink. Indeed, free wine is one of the promises of salvation (Isa. 55:1; Luke 22:18). Thus the psalmist praised God for making "the wine that gladdens the heart of man" (Ps. 104:15). Obviously he was talking about something more potent than grape juice, which may be nice to drink but never exactly gladdened anyone's heart. And speaking of glad hearts, who could ever forget the wedding at Cana, where Jesus turned water into fine wine (John 2:1–11)? But then, as a matter of principle, Jesus never was a teetotaler, which perhaps explains why his enemies accused him of being a "drunkard" (Matt. 11:19).

At the same time that the Bible gives us the liberty to drink alcohol, however, it also gives many strong warnings about the dangers of its abuse. God knows how easy it is for liberty to become an excuse for license, especially when it comes to drinking. The prophet Isaiah pronounced "woe to those who . . . stay up late at night till they are inflamed with wine" (Isa. 5:11; cf. Prov. 23:29–35).

If anything, the New Testament is even stronger in its warnings against inebriation. When it lists the sins we need to avoid—the sins that will prevent us from seeing God's glory—it often includes the sin of drunkenness. "The acts of the sinful nature are obvious," Paul reminded the Galatians, "sexual immorality, impurity and debauchery; idolatry and witchcraft . . . drunkenness, orgies, and the like." Then he closes with this admonition: "I warn you, as I did before, that those who live like this will not inherit the kingdom of God" (Gal. 5:19–21; cf. 1 Peter 4:3).

If alcohol was dangerous in biblical times, it is even more dangerous today. For one thing, we now know more about the harmful effects that alcohol can have on the body, which for the Christian is "a temple of the Holy Spirit" (1 Cor. 6:19). For another thing, the people of biblical times did not drive automobiles. We do, and thus we face the mortal danger of drunk driving.

Furthermore, alcoholic beverages are more readily available now than at almost any time in human history. Beer, wine, vodka, whiskey—it's all available at the corner bar or the local liquor store. It has never been easier to get drunk than it is right now in America, which also means it has never been easier to become an alcoholic. People often describe alcoholism as a disease. It is more helpful to call the abuse of alcohol a sin and at the same time to recognize it as a sin that enslaves the body as well as the soul.

To summarize, the biblical position on alcohol is liberty without license. Christians are free to drink a modicum of wine and other beverages. They are also free not to drink. As a matter of prudence, Christians who have escaped from bondage to alcohol often find it better not to drink. This too is a way of exercising Christian freedom, for we have as much liberty *not* to drink as we have to drink.

However we exercise our liberty, we must be careful to avoid alcohol license. Here are some practical guidelines:

First, be careful about the company you keep. Many young people face a great deal of pressure to party, especially on weekends. The temptation may even come from friends who claim to be Christians. But here are some questions to ask about the people we hang out with: Are my friendships drawing me closer to God or are they slowing me down in my spiritual progress? Am I influencing my friends for Christ or are they influencing me? Remember that "friendship with the world is hatred toward God" (James 4:4). Do not listen to anyone who says to "take life easy; eat, drink and be merry" (Luke 12:19). Jesus said that people who say such things are fools—not because there is anything wrong with eating, drinking, or being merry—but because they have a frivolous and unspiritual attitude toward life.

Second, if having a drink seems important to you, then it's too important. A Christian liberty is something to be enjoyed but never something to be insisted upon. If we find ourselves craving a drink, if we feel as if we must have one to be happy, then we are no longer at liberty. Alcohol is becoming our master, and it is time to rebel against it.

Another practical guideline for preventing our liberty from becoming license is to examine why we are having a drink. Sometimes people drink in order to loosen their inhibitions. That is not a spiritual impulse. The apostle Paul said, "Do not get drunk on wine, which leads to debauchery. Instead, be filled with the Spirit" (Eph. 5:18). In other words, the best and truest joy comes from being who we are in Christ and not from some artificial stimulant. When we are full of God's Spirit, we are content with who we are. But without the Spirit, it is tempting to turn to a different kind of "spirits" in order to be happy, especially in social situations.

The last practical guideline is to remember that intoxication impairs a person's judgment. The writer of Ecclesiastes described his youth as a time when he was "cheering [himself] with wine, and embracing folly" (Eccles. 2:3). Have you been cheering yourself with wine or with some other alcoholic beverage? Anyone who drinks to excess embraces folly. Strong drink often leads people to say and to do things that it would have been better to leave unsaid and undone. The book of Proverbs says that "wine is a mocker" (Prov. 20:1)—it makes a fool out of the person who drinks too much. Heed the Bible's warning, and don't let alcohol license make a fool out of you!

38

NOT WORTH
THE GAMBLE

*I*t didn't seem serious at the beginning. A number of high school friends started guessing which National Football League teams were going to win each week and throwing a dollar into the pot for the best guesser. Then it was NCAA basketball, and guys were talking about giving and taking points, whatever that meant. Then it was the National Hockey League playoffs, and even some of the girls were paying money and talking about their picks. Still, it didn't seem all that serious.

By senior year there was a regular weekly poker game and the stakes were getting bigger. But seven days is a long time to wait to feed an addiction, so guys started playing cards in the cafeteria at lunchtime, hiding them under the table. Even then it didn't seem too serious.

It seemed a lot more serious several years later, when I heard that one of my classmates had a serious gambling problem. He was down at the racetrack, playing the horses. He couldn't hold down a steady job, and everybody was sad about it. It was only then that I realized that gambling is a destructive addiction.

A 1996 report to the Philadelphia City Council recognized some of the dangers of that addiction.[1] The idea of bringing riverboat gambling to the Delaware River had refused to die, so then–City Council President John Street commissioned a report on the social costs of casino gambling. Among other things, the report warned of the dangers of an influx of compulsive gamblers and an unhealthy alliance between government and the gaming industry. The connections between gambling and social ills—like prostitution, divorce, and child abuse—are widely known.

It turns out that riverboat gambling may not even be good economics. Casinos usually fail to meet financial expectations. The apparent advantages of new jobs and increased revenues are offset by the subtraction of dollars from other forms of entertainment, like sports and movies. Furthermore, the cost to the public of the average pathological gambler is in the neighborhood of fifteen thousand dollars. At least, that's how much the public paid in 1981, due to theft, embezzlement, and the judicial costs necessitated by gambling.

Gambling has become even bigger business since then. What was a ten-billion-dollar-a-year concern in 1982 has since become a more than forty-billion-dollar-a-year industry.[2] As gambling continues to expand, unscrupulous politicians are bound to turn to dice and cards for salvation. After every election, we can expect politicians to make a good return on the campaign contributions they received from the gambling industry by introducing new casino legislation.

The church has long recognized the dangers of gambling. Already in the third century, Tertullian observed that "if you say you are a Christian when you are a dice-player, you say you are what you are not, for you are a partner with the world."3 The Westminster Divines didn't go into the subject at length, but they did warn about the dangers of "wasteful gaming."4

Gambling is a sin for a number of reasons.5 First, it denies God's providence. God promises to provide everything we need (Phil. 4:19), but he doesn't tell us to gamble to get it. The providence of God does not need to be helped along by lottery tickets or sweepstakes entries. Instead, the Bible teaches us that God provides daily bread in abundance, as we work for it (1 Thess. 4:11–12).

Second, gambling is bad stewardship. Everything that we are and have belongs to God (Rom. 8:14; Ps. 24:1), and it has been given to us to meet our needs and to bring glory to God. But gambling puts what belongs to God at risk; it jeopardizes what God has entrusted to our care. In the parable of the talents, the wicked servant is chastised for failing to put his talent on deposit (Matt. 25:27), not for failing to take it to the bingo parlor.

Third, gambling is stealing. Every form of gambling is an attempt to profit from someone else's loss. There are always winners, but there are also losers, and there are usually a lot more losers than winners. That's why it's a gamble!

The fact that the victims of gambling are usually anonymous does not legitimize the vice. It is often observed that lotteries are a way of stealing from the poor to give to the rich. That seemed to be the case when I was in Haiti, where the lotto stands are especially common in the poorest communities. This phenomenon makes me wonder about the marketing slogan used by the Pennsylvania State Lottery: "Benefits Older Pennsylvanians." Maybe, but at whose expense?

Fourth, gambling comes from coveting. In his famous "Sermons on the Cards," the seventeenth-century Anglican bishop Jeremy Taylor (1613–1667) put it this way: "If a man be willing or indifferent to lose his own money and not at all desirous to get another's, to what purpose is it that he plays for it? If he be not indifferent, then he is covetous."6 In other words, if you're not in it for the money, then why gamble? And if you are in it for the money, then you're coveting.

A man once came to Jesus with a financial problem. It wasn't a gambling problem, but the man wanted Jesus to tell his brother to give him half of his inheritance. This is the warning Jesus gave to him, and to everyone who is willing to gamble for a bigger slice of the pie: "Watch out! Be on your guard against all kinds of greed; a man's life does not consist in the abundance of possessions" (Luke 12:15).

39

ROAD RAGE

*I*n some Christian circles, a distinction is drawn between application and meddling. When the pastor preaches against the sins of others, that's application. When he stings your own conscience, that's meddling. As a pastor I try to do my share of meddling. I am almost certain to do it here, unless you are wise enough to live without an automobile, because I want to talk about your driving habits.

Are you an aggressive driver? Here is how the *Philadelphia Inquirer* describes them:

> Aggressive drivers tend to be easily frustrated and show little concern for fellow motorists. They run stop signs and red lights, speed, tailgate, weave in and out of traffic, pass on the right, make

improper and unsafe lane changes, use hand gestures, scream, honk and flash their lights. Some dislike being passed and will speed up to cut off another driver.[1]

Do any of these driving habits sound familiar? Anyone who commutes encounters aggressive drivers every day.

Road rage has become a national problem. Miles driven are up by one-third. So is the blood pressure of the average motorist. According to one survey, 80 percent of American drivers say they are angry all or most of the time they are in the car. As a result, angry motorists killed more than two hundred people in 1997. Perhaps not surprisingly, road rage was used as a legal defense in a recent criminal trial, even though the judge didn't buy it.

The problem has become so serious that the American Automobile Association (AAA) is trying to do something about it. The AAA Foundation for Traffic Safety has released a report on aggressive driving. Among other things, AAA recommends avoiding eye contact with angry drivers, letting other people pass, laying off the horn, and refusing to return uncomplimentary gestures.

This is wise counsel. It also raises a question: How should Christians drive? A friend of mine asked me that question not long after he became a Christian. In the fervor of his newfound faith in Jesus Christ he had purchased a decorative fish at his local Christian bookstore and attached it to his trunk. (The fish is an ancient symbol of Christianity.) A few weeks later some of his friends asked him to unhook his fish. They said his driving was a poor testimony. If he was going to drive like a pagan, they explained, it would be better not to advertise for Jesus.

So how should Christians drive? First, Christians should drive safely, which includes observing the speed limit. This is something we owe to the governing authorities, which have been established by God: "He who rebels against the authority is rebelling against what God has instituted, and those who do so will bring judgment on themselves" (Rom. 13:2). Safe driving is also something we owe to our neighbors. Reckless driving violates the sixth commandment: "Thou shalt not kill" (Ex. 20:13 KJV). Worldwide, half a million people are killed in automobile accidents every year. People who drive carefully preserve their lives, the lives of their passengers, and the lives of other motorists.

Christians should also drive patiently. This is not easy because automobiles feed our lust for power. Urbanologist David Engwicht explains what happens to us when we slide behind the wheel: "Metamorphosis takes place as the driver is transformed from homo-sapiens to homo-machine, both hearts of steel united in their drive for efficiency, speed, and power. The driver becomes the driven."[2] Cars give the illusion of power. In addition to controlling a car's speed, drivers have seat control, sound control, and climate control. But speed, comfort, and power easily become idols. Driving a car is a way of seeking mastery over time and space. We want to get where we are going sooner rather than later, and we don't want anyone to get in our way.

These attitudes are signs of idolatry. Notice the reaction whenever our mastery over time and space is thwarted. What happens to our blood pressure when we are running late or get stuck in traffic? How do we respond when we get cut off, or when the lanes narrow, or when we have trouble finding a parking spot? We get angry. Of course we do! Anger is the natural response when we are kept from our gods.

The thing to realize when we start beating on our steering wheels in frustration is that we have a spiritual problem. The real problem is not the driver in front of us or the traffic jam on the interstate; the real problem is in our hearts.

The way we drive is a good test of our godliness. We do not cease to be children of God when we put the key in the ignition. We are not anonymous motorists; we are Christian motorists. So be gracious. Let other people go first. Be patient and forgiving toward the sins of other drivers.

Sanctified driving is especially important for parents. We are teaching our children how to drive every time we get behind the wheel. We may also be teaching them hostility. "What's that guy's problem?" one of my regular passengers once asked. It was a rotten thing to say, but it hardly seemed fair to blame the child for repeating what he had sometimes heard from his father!

I commend the Christian virtue that is most useful for driving: patience. If we have trouble being patient, it might be good to put this paraphrase on the dashboard: "I urge you to drive your car worthy of the calling you have received. Be completely humble and gentle; be patient, bearing with other motorists in love" (Eph. 4:1–2).

40

CHEATERS NEVER
PROSPER

*I*n 1996 a survey was taken at Villanova University to determine the extent of cheating on campus. The results astounded even the most cynical academics: 89 percent of Villanova students admitted cheating at least once during their years in college. Eighty-nine percent! And this at an institution shaped by Christian values.

The Villanova survey was part of a nationwide study by the Center for Academic Integrity.[1] The national statistics were disturbing. Sixty-three percent of American students admitted cheating on an exam and 80 percent on a writing assignment. The figures were lower at institutions with an honor code, but not much lower. Even at colleges and universities with an honor code, four in ten students cheated on exams and six in ten on written assignments.

What counts as cheating? The survey listed a wide range of academic sins: copying off someone else's test, using crib notes, obtaining questions or answers in advance, plagiarism, falsifying lab data, and collaborating without a professor's permission. Sin is like that; there are usually lots of ways to do it.

Cheating is nothing new. In the 1980s I spent several weeks at a summer high school debate institute at the University of Iowa. While I was there I overheard several college students talking about the elaborate system they had for cheating on exams. They were fraternity brothers, and their fraternity had a complete file of old examinations. Cheating is even more sophisticated now that it is possible to download term papers off the Internet.

The temptation to cheat can be overwhelming, especially when everybody's doing it. The pressure to succeed is enormous. Prospects for jobs and further education depend largely on success in college. Students are burdened with the expectations of their parents, not to mention their own expectations.

I can still remember the time in high school when I was most tempted to cheat on an exam. I went into the basketball coach's classroom to take an American history test I had missed during an illness. One of the questions was a stumper about one of our early American presidents. As I was puzzling over the answer I suddenly remembered that there was a poster of the U.S. presidents on the wall immediately behind me. All I needed to do was turn around and read the answer.

Later, I almost wished I had. When I pointed out to the coach that he had left the answer on the bulletin board, he said, "Hey, if I'm stupid enough to give you the answer, go ahead and take it." But I was right not to look. Christians need to be scrupulously honest in their academic work.

Cheating violates at least three of the Ten Commandments. First, it is stealing and therefore violates the eighth commandment: "Thou shalt not steal" (Ex. 20:15 KJV). To cheat is to take something that does not belong to us: an answer, a quotation, a lab result.

Second, cheating is lying and therefore violates the ninth commandment: "Thou shalt not bear false witness against thy neighbor" (Exod. 20:16 KJV). Cheating is false witness because it misrepresents our knowledge of a particular subject. We are lying about what we know. The lie is compounded where an honor code is in place, because we have given our word of honor not to cheat. Cheating is a sin against our neighbor because it puts him or her at a disadvantage, particularly if grading is done on the curve. Cheating is not a victimless crime; it damages every other student in the class.

Finally, for Christians, cheating violates the third commandment: "Thou shalt not take the name of the LORD thy God in vain" (Ex. 20:7 KJV). As Christians we bear the name of Christ. We are his representatives in the world. Everything we do is a reflection on his name and character. When we cheat, we bring dishonor to his name as well as our own. Cheating is a great sin, especially because it is a secret sin.

Students who have cheated should give their consciences no rest until they make full confession of their sin to the Lord. "If we confess our sins, he is faithful and just and will forgive us our sin and purify us from all unrighteousness" (1 John 1:9). Cheaters also need to confess their sin to the teacher or professor in charge. True repentance means turning away from sin and everything we have gained by it.

Even students who think they do all their academic work with complete integrity should consider whether they study with all their heart, soul, mind, and strength (Mark 12:30). Students show their love for God by the way they do their art, their humanities, or their science. An easel, a desk, or a lab table ought to be an altar of praise. Therefore to do anything less than our best work is to cheat God. There is a sharp difference between doing our best and doing well enough to get by. Students who write term papers at 3:00 a.m., pop No-Doz, and take coffee intravenously, are not offering the Lord their best work.

What student or what worker can honestly say that he or she has not cheated God? This is why we are in such great need of the gospel. The best that we offer to God, even in the area of our best talents, bears the smudge of our sin. We are cheaters by nature, which is why we are in constant, daily need of the cleansing power of the blood of Jesus Christ.

41

THAT DEMON, SPORT

The Christians at Gilcomston South Church in Aberdeen, Scotland, know how to pray. Every Saturday night sixty or seventy of them gather in the church hall to spend two hours praying for the work of the gospel around the world.

One Saturday night I heard a church leader pray against the rulers and dominions of spiritual darkness in the city of Aberdeen. He prayed against the principalities of corruption, drinking, gambling, materialism, and prostitution. "And especially," he continued, "that demon, sport."

"Wait a second," I thought. "Was it my imagination, or did that man just pray against 'that demon, sport'? I'm not sure I'm familiar with that demon!"

I don't really know if Satan has assigned one or more demons to rule over the wide world of sports, but I do know that sports have spiritual power. Sports, like every other good thing, can become idols. Every January millions of Americans gather for our nation's most important religious exercise: the Super Bowl. When I speak of the Super Bowl as a religious event I am not trying to be humorous. Super Bowl Sunday receives the kind of analysis and attention that only a god can command. The worshiping community that gathers around a television set at a Super Bowl party is a sort of counterfeit house church.

The trouble with sports, like other idols, is that they always disappoint their worshipers. One fall Philadelphians were basking in the afterglow of an Eagles' victory in Dallas. The following Friday I taught a Bible study on the subject of idolatry. "Almost anything can become an idol," I said at a certain point, "even the Philadelphia Eagles." I heard a groan beside me as a young lawyer in the study said, "I was hoping you wouldn't say that."

I returned to the study a month later. When the lawyer greeted me, he said, "You know, Phil, the Eagles haven't won a game since you told us they could become an idol." "Hey, it's not my fault," I protested. "That's the way idols are: they always let you down." The problem with false gods is that they always leave us hungry for more. They cannot satisfy.

Nor can they save. At the beginning of one football season something tragic happened before a game. The Philadelphia Eagles' most loyal fan, a man who had attended every home game for decades, was to be interviewed on the radio. Just minutes before he was scheduled to go on the air he had a massive heart attack and died. Although his friends and family were sad, they said over and over again how appropriate it was for him to die at the stadium. "He was in his glory!" one of his friends said. Those words haunted me for weeks. Some glory! He was the kind of man described in Romans 1:23, a man who "exchanged the glory of the immortal God for images made to look like . . . birds" (Rom. 1:23).

There are at least two good ways to tell when a sport is in danger of becoming an idol. One is to notice how tense we get when we are watching a big game or how upset we get when our team loses. Our emotions reveal where our heart has placed its ultimate loyalties.

Another way to tell if sports are becoming idolatrous is to keep track of the time and money we spend playing and watching sports. Are sports distracting us from more important activities like Bible reading or talking with our children? If so, there is something idolatrous about our sporting activities.

Roger Angell, who is one of America's best baseball writers, has this to say about the place sports have come to occupy in our culture:

> Sports are too much with us. Late and soon, sitting and watch-ing—mostly watching on television—we lay waste our powers of identification and enthusiasm . . . as more and more closing rallies and crucial putts and late field goals and final playoffs and sudden deaths and world records and world championships unreel them-selves ceaselessly before our half-lidded eyes. Professional leagues expand like bubble gum, ever larger and thinner, and the extended sporting seasons, now bunching and overlapping at the ends, con-clude in exhaustion and the wrong weather. . . . The American ob-session with sports is not a new phenomenon, of course, except in its . . . excessive excessiveness. What *is* new . . . is a curious sense of loss. In the midst of all these successive spectacles and instant replays and endless reportings and recapitulations, we seem to have forgotten what we came for.[1]

It is worth noting that Angell wrote these words in 1972. In the last thirty years everything he laments has gotten worse. There are more sports, more leagues, more teams, more games, and more replays.

At the same time, there is much less of what sports are for in the first place: play. Sports do not have to become idols. What keeps them from be-coming idols is playing them to the glory of God. There is space for sports in the Christian life, the same space God gives us for other forms of play.

There are sports to play in the kingdom of God. One of the most beau-tiful promises about the new Jerusalem is found in Zechariah 8, where the

Lord promises that "the city streets will be filled with boys and girls playing there" (Zech. 8:5). Surely some of these children play sports. I have always imagined them playing stickball, but it might be jacks, or hopscotch,
or roller hockey, or basketball. Who knows? But whatever they are playing, God's children are not under the spell of that demon, sport. They are
playing to the glory of God.

42

FOOT AND MOUTH
(AND HEART)

*L*ike most of the arguments people have with God, Jonah's dispute over the fate of the godless city of Nineveh ended with God getting the last word. Jonah had told the Ninevites to repent or perish. Secretly he hoped that they would perish; but to his dismay, they repented. While Jonah was sulking, God said to him, "Nineveh has more than a hundred and twenty thousand people who cannot tell their right hand from their left, and many cattle as well. Should I not be concerned about that great city?" (Jonah 4:11).

Jonah was surprised to learn that God cared so much for Nineveh. But what surprises me is that he also cared about the cattle. God's primary concern was for lost souls—more than one hundred thousand Ninevites. Yet he was also concerned about what happened to their cows.

This gives some indication how Christians should respond to the crisis faced in recent years by European cattle and other livestock. For more than a decade we have been hearing about the dangers of mad cow disease (*bovine spongiform encephalopathy*, or BSE). Recent attention has also turned to an epidemic of foot and mouth disease (FMD), a highly contagious infection that affects cattle and other animals with cloven hooves. As recently as 1995, Europe was virtually free of foot and mouth disease, which probably explains why European livestock are now so vulnerable to the disease.

The symptoms of foot and mouth disease are distressing. As a result of painful blisters on their mouths and noses, cattle suffer salivation, anorexia, and lameness. Because the disease is so contagious, measures for its containment are drastic. When a contaminated animal is discovered, all of the livestock on the same farm are slaughtered. Furthermore, because the virus is windborne, livestock on adjacent farms are also killed. In Britain one outbreak was so severe that the British army began digging huge pits for the mass burning and burial of hundreds of thousands of cows, pigs, and sheep. According to some estimates, well over one million animals were slaughtered before the disease was brought under control.

Although some measures are taken to prevent an outbreak of foot and mouth disease in this country, most Americans are relatively unconcerned. It is typical for us not to care much about problems that do not seem to affect us directly. Besides, unlike mad cow disease, foot and mouth disease does not infect humans. So in human terms, the effect of the disease is primarily economic, with losses running into the tens of millions of dollars.

Shouldn't we be more concerned? In fact, as Christians, would it not be appropriate for us to lament this tremendous loss of animal life?

It would help if we had a more robust theology of creation. The Bible has a great deal to say about animals in general and about cattle in particular. For starters, we know that God is the one who made the cattle. God said, "Let the land produce living creatures according to their kinds: livestock, creatures that move along the ground, and wild animals, each according to its kind" (Gen. 1:24). We also know why God made cattle. Like everything else he made, it was for his glory. Thus the psalmist invites all the cattle to praise the name of the Lord (Ps. 148:7–13). This does not mean that we should consider cows sacred, the way that Hindus do, but we should respect them for the sake of their Creator.

God not only made the cattle, but in his providence he also takes care of them. Asaph said that God owns "the cattle on a thousand hills" (Ps. 50:10). Since they are his livestock, "he makes grass grow for the cattle, and plants for man to cultivate—bringing forth food from the earth" (Ps. 104:14). Elsewhere the Bible identifies the flourishing of livestock as a blessing from God (Deut. 11:15; 28:4; Ps. 107:38; Isa. 30:23). But in order for cattle to flourish, they need the care of their owners. Thus the Bible commends the righteous man for providing for the needs of his animals (Prov. 12:10). Human beings have a duty of care for their animals, including livestock. This explains why God included farm animals in the fourth commandment, providing for their Sabbath rest (Ex. 20:10).

Like everything else in creation, cattle suffer the effects of the fall. On occasion, they endure the effects of divine judgment. Such was the case in Egypt, when, as a result of Pharaoh's sin, livestock were plagued with disease and death (Ex. 9:1–7, 25; 12:29; cf. Hag. 1:11). More often cattle are mistreated through neglect or exploitation. Some modern ranches are run more like factories than farms. Livestock are not allowed to roam free, following the normal patterns of animal behavior, but are crammed together for force feeding. Even foot and mouth disease may be considered the result of the fall, for it was sin that first brought disease into the world.

The suffering of cattle is one small part of what the Bible means when it says that "the creation was subjected to frustration" (Rom. 8:20) and that "the whole creation has been groaning as in the pains of childbirth right up to the present time" (Rom. 8:22). The cattle groan because, like everything else that God has created, they are waiting to be "liberated from [their] bondage to decay" (Rom. 8:21). If the cattle are groaning as the result of our sin, then it is right for us to raise a lament and sometimes even to pray, not only for cattle farmers but also for their cattle.

43

I WAS IN PRISON

*W*hen I first came to Philadelphia's Tenth Presbyterian Church, I was somewhat surprised to discover that the congregation did not have a prison ministry. I recalled the parable of the sheep and the goats, in which Jesus described the good deeds that the early church called "the six acts of charity": feeding the hungry, satisfying the thirsty, housing the stranger, clothing the naked, caring for the sick, and visiting the imprisoned (Matt. 25:35–39). The point of the parable is that those who practice such acts of mercy minister to Christ (Matt. 25:40), while those who fail to practice them will be condemned to eternal punishment (Matt. 25:41–46). In one way or another Tenth Church was doing all these things, except visiting prisoners. Hence my surprise.

I later learned that the reason we did not have a prison ministry was primarily due to lack of opportunity. Our mercy ministries concentrate on the needs of our urban community, and there were no long-term prison facilities nearby.

Now we have a group of volunteers trained to conduct Bible studies, lead worship services, and establish spiritually beneficial friendships at the Federal Detention Center opened in 2000. Their training was conducted by Prison Fellowship, the national prison ministry founded by Charles Colson, with additional orientation provided by prison staff.

The need for prison ministry has never been greater. The United States is number one in the world in terms of incarceration rate.[1] Nearly two million Americans are now in prison, a figure that has doubled in the last fifteen years. Half of these persons end up in maximum-security correctional facilities, where they face overcrowding, violence, rape, and homicide. It is not surprising that many prisoners struggle with depression, drug abuse, boredom, and fear. Despite these difficulties, of the inmates who are ultimately released, more than half will end up back in prison within two years.

It is often thought that prisoners get what they deserve. It is true that, despite all the imperfections of the American justice system, most inmates do time for crimes they have committed. But this is no reason to abandon them. If the good news about Jesus Christ is for undeserving sinners, then what better place to take the gospel than to prison?

Prison ministry is not easy. At first, most volunteers are apprehensive about going into prison. Usually there are significant experiential barriers that make it hard to establish friendships with the residents. Volunteers may have concerns about their personal safety, and they must always be on their guard against manipulation.

But it is just because prison ministry is so difficult that it is so necessary. It is necessary because it exposes some of the most serious problems facing our nation.

One reason we have so many prisoners is because America has such a serious crime problem. Every day some thirty thousand assaults are committed on our nation's streets. Our crime problem is also an economic problem. The total annual price tag on crime in America is placed at around seven hundred billion dollars. But the ultimate problem is not economic or even criminal but spiritual. The despair that we find in our nation's prisons finds its origin in the sins of the human heart. The real captivity is the prison house of sin. Colson writes, "Prison ministry is on the frontline of church service today, because prisons are the place where we are coming face-to-face with an evil that threatens to destroy us."

By confronting this evil, prison ministry shows the church and the world that no one is beyond God's mercy. "When the steel door of that prison cell crashes behind you," said one prisoner, "something dies inside. You lose your name. You become a number. No one knows who you are. No one cares." Prison ministry proves that God knows and cares about those whom everyone else has forgotten.

Prison ministry is also necessary to show that the gospel of Jesus Christ has the power to effect spiritual change. In the words of one volunteer,

> When someone is in prison, they are at the lowest point in their lives. Their whole world collapses into the space between those guarded walls. Visiting week after week, getting to know them, you begin to break through some even tougher walls . . . walls of bitterness, remorse, anger and despair. The day comes when they have to ask, "Why are you here? Why do you care?" That's when you tell them about Jesus. That's when lives change.

Jesus came to set the captives free (see Isa. 42:7; 61:1), and if he can change the life of a hardened criminal, he can change anyone.

Finally, prison ministry is necessary because Christ commanded it. This does not mean that we have to visit a prisoner to be saved. But it does mean that a church with a prison in its neighborhood cannot be faithful to the cause of Christ unless it is willing to take the gospel to prison. If Christians do take the gospel to prison, then on the day when Christ comes into his kingdom and the sheep are separated from the goats, they will hear Jesus say, "I was in prison and you came to visit me" (Matt. 25:36b).

PART 7

FEASTS AND FESTIVALS

The most festive festival it is possible to celebrate is divine worship. And there is no festival that does not draw its vitality from worship and that has not become a festival by virtue of its origin in worship. . . . It is true that . . . attempts have been made to manufacture feast days and holidays that have no connection with divine worship. . . . In point of fact the stress and strain of giving them some kind of festal appearance is one of the very best proofs of the significance of divine worship for a feast.

—JOSEF PIEPER

The major Christian holidays—Thanksgiving, Christmas, and Easter—still have their hold on American religion. Christmas and Easter celebrate two great events in the life of Jesus Christ: his incarnation and his resurrection (and if Good Friday is included with Easter, also his crucifixion). Thanksgiving is not directly tied to the person and work of Christ. Yet it is properly considered a Christian holiday because, as one of the essays in this section explains, it has its origins in the worship of the Puritans.

In an increasingly post-Christian society, these holidays continue to stimulate a good deal of religious fervor. Many Americans still consider

Thanksgiving a day for giving thanks to God. There are still Christmas-and-Easter Christians who go to church only on these two days each year. And during the holiday season Americans are more likely to think about God, to pray, and to watch religious programming on television.

Paradoxically these holidays are also the most profane times of the year. I use the word *profane* in its technical sense, as the misuse of something holy. Thanksgiving may be a time to give thanks, but these days it is also a time to get stuffed. And when Americans do give thanks, they are more likely to give it to some amorphous supreme deity than to the God and Father of our Lord Jesus Christ.

Christmas is even worse. With all the reindeer, tinsel, and the wrapping paper, it is hard to find the manger scene, let alone the Christ child. Christians can see the vast chasm between the incarnation and its reincarnation at the postmodern shopping mall. Often we are tempted to say what Mary said outside the empty tomb: "They have taken my Lord away . . . and I don't know where they have put him" (John 20:13b)!

Given what has happened to the holidays, it is not hard to understand why the Puritans were so resistant to celebrating them. They instinctively sensed the potential danger of turning the gospel into a sideshow. In some ways, Thanksgiving and Christmas are the hardest times of the year for people to hear the message of salvation. There is too much background noise, and often the message that does come through is badly distorted.

Still, the holidays are a time when many people are more likely to think about spiritual things. This gives Christians an extraordinary opportunity to share their faith, to introduce people to Jesus Christ. Perhaps these essays will help you know what to say and how to say it.

44

TALKING TURKEY

*O*ne of my favorite football announcers insists on calling Thanksgiving "Turkey Day." Whenever he does, I bristle at the way he tries to make the sacred secular.

Thanksgiving Day was never intended to be a secular activity. The Pilgrims who gathered at Plymouth to celebrate the first Thanksgiving in 1621 did so because they wanted to thank God for a good harvest after a harsh winter. Likewise, when the Continental Congress met during the 1770s and 1780s, they set apart an annual day of Thanksgiving so that the American people might give thanks

> above all, that [God] hath diffused the glorious light of the gospel, whereby, through the merits of our gracious Redeemer, we may become the heirs of his eternal glory.

Such days were not for thanksgiving alone. The stated intent was that

> together with their sincere acknowledgments and offerings, [the American people] may join the penitent confession of their manifold sins, whereby they had forfeited every favour, and their humble and earnest supplication that it may please God, through the merits of Jesus Christ, mercifully to forgive and blot them out of remembrance.[1]

When George Washington announced a national Day of Thanksgiving in 1789, he did so with thanksgiving to God clearly in mind. He declared:

> Whereas it is the duty of all nations to acknowledge the providence of Almighty God, to obey His will, to be grateful for His benefits, and humbly implore his protection and favor. . . . Now therefore I do recommend and assign Thursday the twenty-sixth of November next, to be devoted by the people of these States to the service of that Great and Glorious Being . . . that we may then all unite in rendering unto Him our sincere and humble thanks for His kind care and protection of the people of this country; . . . for the great degree of tranquility, union and plenty which we have . . . enjoyed; . . . for the civil and religious liberty with which we are blessed; . . . and in general, for all the great and various favors which He has been pleased to confer upon us.[2]

Not long afterwards, beginning with the Jefferson administration, America came down with a case of Thanksgiving amnesia. National celebration of Thanksgiving was sporadic during the first half of the nineteenth century, when Sarah J. Hale finally convinced Abraham Lincoln of the necessity of celebrating such a day every year.

Thanksgiving has been celebrated in America ever since. And yet we now suffer from a different strain of Thanksgiving amnesia, not forgetting the day but forgetting the God who deserves our thanks. Thanksgiving has gradually been reduced from Thanksgiving Day to Turkey Day, from a spiritual activity to a culinary activity, from a focus on the goodness of God and the grace of Christ to a focus on dark meat and white meat.

What's the first thing that comes to mind when we think of Thanksgiving? Turkey? The Detroit Lions? Family? Or do we think first and foremost of the God in whom food and football and family all find their ultimate purpose?

True thanksgiving is more than just a vague feeling of well-being, a general satisfaction with life, and a full tummy. Whenever we give thanks, we are giving thanks to someone. Thank-you notes always have addresses on them. And if we're not careful to remember whom we are thanking, we run the risk of stuffing ourselves with self-congratulation.

The Bible teaches that thanksgiving is a perpetual activity for the people of God. Psalm 100:4 reads, "Enter his gates with thanksgiving and his courts with praise; give thanks to him and praise his name." In Philippians 4:6 we read, "In everything, by prayer and petition, with thanksgiving, present your requests to God." Or consider 1 Thessalonians 5:18: "Give thanks in all circumstances, for this is God's will for you in Christ Jesus." The Old Testament people of God regularly brought thank offerings to the temple. In Psalm 50:23, the Lord says, "He who sacrifices thank offerings honors me, and he prepares the way so that I may show him the salvation of God."

The Bible teaches that in addition to ongoing and perpetual thanksgivings, special seasons of thanksgiving are beneficial for the people of God. Noah celebrated the first Thanksgiving when he praised God for delivering him from the flood and offered sweet-smelling sacrifices to the Lord (Gen. 8:20–21). After the children of Israel were delivered from Egypt, they had several annual thanksgiving feasts. They celebrated both at the beginning and at the end of harvest, giving thanks to God at the Feast of Firstfruits (e.g., Lev. 23:9–14) and the Feast of Weeks (e.g., Num. 28:26–31). The

Feast of Tabernacles (e.g., Num. 29:12–34) and the Feast of Passover (e.g., Num. 9:1–14) were also festivals of thanksgiving to God.

Thus it is nonsense for the *Encyclopedia Britannica* to suggest that the American Thanksgiving Day is "rooted in native tradition." Thanksgiving is rooted in biblical tradition.

That biblical tradition was preserved and passed down to the American church by the Presbyterian churches of England and Scotland. The ministers who wrote the Westminster Confession of Faith (1643–1646) were well aware of the biblical precedent for thanksgiving festivals. So they included an entire section in *The Directory for the Publick Worship of God* on thanksgiving, entitled "Of the Observation of Days of Publick Thanksgiving." They instructed ministers that "when any such day is to be kept, let notice be given of it, and of the occasion thereof, some convenient time before, that the people may the better prepare themselves thereunto." George Washington and the Continental Congress were adopting this practice when they issued thanksgiving declarations to be read in pulpits throughout the nation.

Mindful of the temptations that a day of feasting might present, the Westminster Divines also gave instructions for the proper conduct of thanksgiving:

> The minister . . . is solemnly to admonish [the congregation] to beware of all excess and riot, tending to gluttony or drunkenness . . . in their eating and refreshing; and to take care that their mirth and rejoicing be not carnal, but spiritual, which may make God's praise to be glorious, and themselves humble and sober; and that both their feeding and rejoicing may render them more cheerful and enlarged, further to celebrate his praises in the midst of the congregation.

These Puritans were not spoilsports. They condemned excess, gluttony, and drunkenness, but they also assumed that thanksgiving to God would entail eating and drinking, mirth and rejoicing, cheerfulness and celebration.

Christians are filled with such mirth and celebration every Thanksgiving. Our rejoicing is not directed toward no one in particular or toward our bellies. Rather, like the Puritans, we intend for our thanks to "make God's praise to be glorious."

45

A WORD OF THANKS

"Go and enjoy choice food and sweet drinks, and send some to those who have nothing prepared. This day is sacred to our LORD."

*D*oes this quotation sound familiar? Who said it? Where is it found?

It sounds like something someone might say on Thanksgiving Day: "Go and enjoy choice food," like turkey and stuffing, potatoes and gravy, cranberry sauce and pumpkin pie. "Go and enjoy . . . sweet drinks," like apple cider and eggnog. "Send some to those who have nothing prepared," like the homeless who come to church for Thanksgiving dinner. "This day is sacred to our LORD," as Thanksgiving always is.

For those who have trouble identifying the quotation, here are a few hints. It comes from the Bible. To be more specific, it comes from the Old Testament. It was spoken by one of the great leaders of Israel, on a day of thanksgiving for God's Word. Here is another hint: the quotation is followed in the Bible by the following words: "Do not grieve, for the joy of the LORD is your strength."

Give up? The quotation comes from Nehemiah, chapter 8. Nehemiah was a cupbearer or wine taster for Artaxerxes, king of Persia. Presumably he knew a thing or two about sweet drinks. In any case, he led God's people back to Jerusalem from their captivity in Babylon.

After the exiles returned to Jerusalem and rebuilt the city wall, they gathered in a city square for the reading of God's law (Neh. 8:1). Ezra the priest stood on a high platform and read the Scriptures aloud from dawn until noon (Neh. 8:3–4). All the people stood up, and whenever Ezra praised the Lord, they lifted their hands and shouted "Amen! Amen!" (Neh. 8:6).

The law of God was not only read; it was also explained. More than a dozen priests stood beside Ezra and "instructed the people in the Law while the people were standing there" (Neh. 8:7). One preacher after another stepped forward to expound the Word of God: "They read from the Book of the Law of God, making it clear and giving the meaning so that the people could understand what was being read" (Neh. 8:8). It was expository preaching at its best.

> Then Nehemiah the governor, Ezra the priest and scribe, and the Levites who were instructing the people said to them all, "This day is sacred to the LORD your God. Do not mourn or weep." For all the people had been weeping as they listened to the words of the Law.
>
> Nehemiah said, "Go and enjoy choice food and sweet drinks, and send some to those who have nothing prepared. This day is sacred to our LORD. Do not grieve, for the joy of the LORD is your strength."

The Levites calmed all the people, saying, "Be still, for this is a sacred day. Do not grieve."

Then all the people went away to eat and drink, to send portions of food and to celebrate with great joy, because they now understood the words that had been made known to them. (Neh. 8:9–12)

These verses teach a number of valuable lessons about thanksgiving. First, they teach how sober it is to live before the face of a holy God. The more the people heard the law of God, the more distressed they became. They brought fresh repentance for sin to their thanksgiving feast.

Second, they teach us to give joyful thanks. Three times the people were commanded not to grieve but to rejoice. For those who trust in God, the joy of salvation always triumphs over sorrow for sin. The tears of repentance are always wiped away by the laughter of forgiveness.

Third, these verses teach that we can eat and drink to the glory of God. Choice food and sweet drinks are good gifts from the hand of God. God not only allows us to celebrate with food and drink; there are times when he positively commands it.

Fourth, they teach us that thanking God includes sharing his good gifts with others. Before we finish the rich feast on our table, we should save at least a few zip-lock bags full of leftovers for the needy. A generous spirit always accompanies a thankful heart.

Finally, these verses teach us to give a word of thanks for the Word of God. The main reason the people of God celebrated with such great joy is because "they now understood the words that had been made known to them" (Neh. 8:12).

Every Thanksgiving, I try to give thanks for the Word of God. I do this because most Monday mornings I wake up empty. However well or badly I have preached the day before, on Monday I am back at square one. When I go to my study later in the morning my computer screen will be blank. In seven days I must preach again and I have nothing to say, absolutely nothing.

I try to savor that empty feeling, because I know how essential it is for me to trust completely for the Lord's help for preaching. I also savor it because I know that by the end of the week I will not be empty but full to the point of overflowing. The Word of God always fills me with good things to say about Jesus Christ.

So I offer this word of thanks for the Word of God. What thanksgiving can you offer to God?

46

THE TRUE MEANING
OF CHRISTMAS

*D*oes Christmas have a "true meaning"? Most of the stories we read and movies we watch at Christmas time teach us that Christmas has a true meaning. It is a meaning that has been lost and forgotten, but thankfully it can be remembered and rediscovered within the space of a thirty-minute television special.

Ebenezer Scrooge discovered the true meaning of Christmas. In Charles Dickens's *A Christmas Carol*, the Ghosts of Christmas Past, Present, and Future come to Mr. Scrooge on Christmas Eve to teach him that the true meaning of Christmas is to give to others rather than keeping everything for himself.

George Bailey discovered the true meaning of Christmas, too. Frank Capra's *It's a Wonderful Life* tells how, in answer to the prayers of his friends and with a little help from an angel trying to earn his wings, George learned that the true meaning of Christmas is that he is needed and loved by his community.

Even the Grinch in Dr. Seuss's *How the Grinch Stole Christmas* discovered the true meaning of Christmas. As he struggled to push his sleigh full of ribbons and tags and boxes and bags back up the mountain, he heard the little Whos down in Whoville welcoming Christmas morning in song. And then he puzzled and puzzled until he discovered that Christmas "*doesn't come from a store*," and "perhaps it means a little bit more."

Those are all valuable lessons to learn. Scrooge, Bailey, and the Grinch are, in their own way, redeemed characters. But the true meaning of Christmas, as it is presented to us at Christmastime, rarely focuses on what the Bible actually teaches about the birth of Jesus Christ. The best exception that proves the rule is the Peanuts Christmas special, which quotes liberally from the Gospel of Luke. Despite our best efforts to the contrary, Christmas tends to become a pagan ritual.

This is the way it has always been. As far as anyone knows, the New Testament Christians did not celebrate Christmas. Neither did the Christians of the early church. In fact, many of the most reliable early church fathers opposed the idea. Tertullian, Jerome, and Augustine all spoke against Christmas because it was scheduled to coincide with Roman celebrations for the sun god. In his *Homilies on Leviticus,* Origen went so far as to assert that only the unregenerate would celebrate such a festival.

During the Reformation, John Calvin (1509–1564) also observed Christmas's tendency toward debauchery and secularism. He agreed with Jerome that it was altogether a bad idea. Similarly, although the Puritans recognized the value of regular Thanksgiving feasts, they were opposed to Christmas feasts. We look in vain in their writings for pithy sayings or warm devotional reflections on the proper celebration of Christmas. The Puritan Parliament went so far as to ban the celebration of Christmas and to forbid the sale of mince pies on December 25. The Westminster Divines had Christmas very much in mind when they wrote that "festival days, vulgarly called *Holy-days*, having no warrant in the word of God, are not to be continued."[1]

What Augustine, Calvin, and the Puritans were worried about is the problem we face today: Christmas has become an essentially pagan ritual. Even for Christians, we must admit, Christmas has become a self-indulgent holiday. The spiritual content of the birth of Jesus Christ has been reduced to a few catchy slogans on the front of Christmas cards at the local Christian bookstore. Even much of the giving we do at Christmas is subject to the rebuke that Jesus gave to the Pharisees when he noticed that they only invited people to dinner who were likely to invite them back. Don't we do much the same thing when we exchange Christmas presents?

The case against Christmas should warn us not to allow Christmas to become a pagan ritual. But there is also a case to be made *for* Christmas. At the same time that we are avoiding becoming pagans, Christmas is an excellent time to invite our pagan friends to become Christians.

In one of his letters, C. S. Lewis (1898–1963) recounted the time that his brother "heard a woman on a 'bus say, as the 'bus passed a church with a Crib [manger] outside it, 'Oh Lor'! They bring religion into everything. Look—they're dragging it even into Christmas now!' "[2]

As a matter of fact, we *do* bring religion into everything, even into matters where religion properly belongs, like Christmas. Because Christmas is a celebration of the birth of Jesus Christ, it is a perfect opportunity to talk about spiritual things. It is a time when people hear religious music, show up at church services, feel the pain of loneliness or family strife, and are reminded of the inability of material possessions to bring lasting joy. These are all spiritual opportunities.

Whether or not Christmas has a true meaning, the incarnation of the Son of God does have a true meaning; it is True with a capital "T." The true meaning of the Son of God becoming man can be found in Philippians 2.

It's a true meaning that has to do with the humiliation of the manger and the cross. It's also a true meaning that has to do with genuine healing and lasting joy for every needy person who comes to Christ. If we choose to think about this true meaning during the Christmas season, that is well and good. And if we also choose to invite others to consider the true meaning of the incarnation, then so much the better.

In a poem entitled "The Advent," Benjamin Breckinridge Warfield (1851–1921), who was Professor of Systematic Theology at Princeton Seminary, wrestled to understand the true meaning of the incarnation. It is a true meaning worth grasping, at Christmas or any other time of the year, for Scrooges and Grinches everywhere:

> The Lord has come into His world!
>   "Nay, nay that cannot be:
> The world is full of noisomeness
>   And all iniquity;
> The Lord—thrice holy is His name—
> He cannot touch this thing of shame."

> The Lord has come into His world!
>   "Ah, then, He comes in might,
> The sword of fury in His hands,
>   With vengeance all bedight!
> O wretched world! thine end draws near,
> Prepare to meet thy God, in fear!"

> The Lord has come into His world!
>   "What! in that baby sweet?
> That broken man, acquaint with grief?
>   Those bleeding hands and feet?
> He is the Lord of all the earth,
> How can He stoop to human birth?"

The Lord has come into His world!
   "A slaughtered Lamb I see,
A smoking altar, on which burns
   A sacrifice for me!
He comes—He comes—O blessed day!—
He comes to take my sin away!"[3]

47

I Shop, Therefore
I Am

I am always a little anxious until I get all my Christmas shopping finished. Typically what happens a few days before Christmas is something like this: With a little help from my daughter Kirsten, I wrap my presents. I still have one or two small items to purchase, but the important thing is that I have made my last trip to the mall. I have finally tracked down the first volume of Patrick O'Brian's Aubrey-Maturin novels and found something suitable for my mother—always the hardest person on my list. I have also purchased a gift for my wife, Lisa. (Often this is something she has picked out for herself, but at least I pay for it.)

I like to get my Christmas shopping done as early as possible. One year

I had a bad experience at Wal-Mart on Christmas Eve, so now I try to go before the toy shelves are empty and the crowds get overwhelming. And the crowds *do* get overwhelming. Anyone who goes shopping the week before Christmas has plenty of company.

At Christmas, more than any other time of year, it becomes obvious that shopping is our national pastime. This is partly because Americans are so rich—richer than ever, in fact. During the last decade of the twentieth century, the median household income rose from thirty-five to fifty-five thousand dollars. Of that fifty-five thousand, the average adult spends one thousand dollars on Christmas presents.

And so we shop. The more money we have, the more money we spend. The more money we spend, the more time we spend at the shopping mall. One might even say that the mall is where Americans go to worship. James Twitchell argues that Americans live to shop.[1] Our current spending spree, Twitchell claims, is not simply the result of a record-breaking stock market; it is a cultural commitment.

In a way, shopping is also a religious commitment. The shopping mall has replaced the church building as the center of our worship. Many of the reasons we shop are religious. We shop to be happy and to feel good, sometimes even to give meaning to our existence. One writer for *Christianity Today* echoed this theme:

> I belong to the Cult of the Next Thing. It's dangerously easy to get enlisted. It happens by default—not by choosing the cult, but by failing to resist it. The Cult of the Next Thing is consumerism cast in religious terms. It has its own litany of sacred words: *more, you deserve it, new, faster, cleaner, brighter.* It has its own deep-rooted liturgy: *charge it, instant credit, no down-payment, deferred payment, no interest for three months.* It has its own preachers, evangelists, prophets, and apostles: ad men, pitchmen, and celebrity sponsors. It has, of course, its own shrines, chapels, temples, meccas: malls, superstores, club warehouses. It has its own sacraments: credit and

debit cards. It has its own ecstatic experiences: the spending spree. The Cult of the Next Thing's central message proclaims, "Crave and spend, for the Kingdom of Stuff is here."[2]

The problem with turning Christmas into a shopping event is not that we miss the true meaning of Christmas; the real danger is missing the true meaning of life. If we do not worship God, we are prone to worship things, especially things that come in shiny packages. Some people worship idols made of wood and stone, but the idols Americans are tempted to worship come wrapped in cellophane and advertised two-for-the-price-of-one.

Given our love for things, it should not surprise us that the beast in Revelation tries to worm his way into the marketplace. Revelation describes what God showed John the Evangelist when he saw heaven opened. One of the things John saw was a beast that "was given authority over every tribe, people, language and nation" (Rev. 13:7b). The Bible says that the beast "forced everyone, small and great, rich and poor, free and slave, to receive a mark on his right hand or on his forehead, so that no one could buy or sell unless he had the mark, which is the name of the beast or the number of his name" (Rev. 13:16–17).

In recent decades, Christians have wasted their time trying to figure out the name of the beast and speculating about his deadly mark: Is it a credit chip surgically attached to the hand, or is it a bar code branded into the forehead? But what really scares us is not so much the mark of the beast, or even the beast himself, but the terrifying prospect of being unable to buy or to sell. The beast knows that the best place to catch us is at the shopping mall. The reason we are in danger of falling under his deadly spell is that we have already sworn allegiance to our consumer culture.

I am not opposed to shopping. There is nothing wrong with buying presents at Christmas, or at any other time of year, for that matter. Gifts are a tangible way of expressing love and friendship. Few experiences in life are as wonderful as receiving a thoughtful gift.

But understand that shopping, like everything else we do, is a spiritual activity. What we buy, and why we buy it, says something about our ultimate spiritual commitments. For example, how many of the gifts we buy are for the poor, for people who are unable to give anything in return? Perhaps it is not surprising that we speak of "exchanging" gifts, which implies that we will get as much as we give. But it is worth remembering that the wise men did not exchange gifts when Jesus was born. Instead they brought their gold, frankincense, and myrrh and laid it all at Jesus' feet.

Someday soon we will all find ourselves waiting in line at the cash register. Before we hand over our credit cards, we would do well to remember that there is more to life than shopping, that we do not belong to the Kingdom of Stuff, that we buy what we buy and give what we give as followers of Jesus Christ.

48

THE TROUBLE
WITH SANTA

One Christmas I started thinking about the way things grow bigger and bigger until they get out of control. It probably started with the tree. We drove to the farm in New Jersey where our church buys its annual Christmas tree. After carefully inspecting virtually every conifer on the property, we finally tagged a blue spruce. It seemed reasonably sized at the time, especially compared with the twenty-five-foot Norway spruce the church was getting. But it looked a lot bigger when it had to be pushed and pulled through the front door and wrestled into a locked and upright position. Thirteen feet of wood, needles, and ornaments—the tree of Babel, I called it.

Big, bigger, and out of control: the same might be said of St. Nicholas. His career began in Patara, Turkey, toward the end of the third century. Nicholas was best known for rescuing three daughters of a destitute nobleman from slavery. As the story goes, he threw three bags of gold through the window so that each daughter would have a suitable dowry. Eventually the day Nicholas died—December 6—came to be regarded as a lucky day, especially for weddings.[1]

Up through the Middle Ages St. Nicholas was a relatively minor saint. He was virtually unknown in colonial America. At the end of the eighteenth century no more than a few Dutch families held a feast of St. Nicholas in early December.

He did not become truly famous until Clement Clarke Moore reinvented him in his famous poem, " 'Twas the Night Before Christmas," which was written in 1822. Moore made the whole thing up: Christmas Eve, the sleigh, the reindeer, the stockings, the presents, the chimney—everything.[2] Moore's poem was widely circulated, and since that time jolly old St. Nick has become one of the most famous fictional characters in history.

What interests me is the way Santa Claus has become a figure of religious devotion. The Santa cult was well under way by the middle of the nineteenth century. Historian Penne Restad explains:

> He served a larger purpose than mere delivery man. Put to work in the domestic sphere, Santa combined characteristics of God, Jesus, and human parents into a presence embodying love, generosity, good humor, and transcendence. Through him, children learned about the rewards of good and bad behavior, and also about the miraculous realities of the invisible world.[3]

Restad is on to something, because Santa has his own theology. Consider his nearly divine attributes. He is omniscient, or all-knowing. He is always watching to see whether children are good or bad. Santa is personal.

Children are encouraged to tell him what they want. They have a relation-ship with him; sometimes they even correspond with him. Santa is also omnipresent, or nearly so. He cannot be all places at once, but somehow he manages to make it down every chimney into every home in the world.

Santa is a judge. He upholds the moral order. First he sees every good and every evil deed, whether open or secret. Then he rewards the righteous and punishes the wicked. Children must behave themselves; otherwise they will end up with a lump of coal in their stockings. As a judge, St. Nick is not very demanding. He is the kind of Santa that liberal theologians would in-vent. He wants us to do our best, but he knows that nobody's perfect.

Once Santa's attributes are recognized, it is easy to see why another historian calls him "a genuinely sacred figure by virtue of his classical heroic traits and his intimate historical and verbal linkage to Christ."[4] Santa even pronounces his own benediction. It is not "peace on earth, goodwill to men," but "Merry Christmas to all, and to all a good night."

The Bible has a word for anyone or anything that gradually occupies the place of God in our lives. It is called an idol. This is the way idols work. They get bigger and bigger until they push God out of his heaven. Or, in this case, until they push Christ out of his manger. The trouble with Santa is that he is too big. He is trying to do a job that only God can do.

Jesus Christ is everything anyone could ever want in a Santa, and more. He alone is the all-knowing, all-present, all-righteous, all-loving God. And not just on Christmas Eve. He is on the job twenty-four hours a day, 365 days a year.

There was a time when at least one member of my household was an ardent believer in Santa Claus. He had all the zeal of a new convert, even after having been asked all the troubling questions: "Where does Santa get *flying* reindeer?" "How can he take presents to *all* the children in one night?" And so on.

Still, he believed without question and beyond doubt. Why? Because, he pointed out, everyone else believes. If Sesame Street believes, the Thanksgiving Day parade believes, and the kids in the neighborhood believe, who can doubt it? "Santa is not just make believe; he's real, Dad!" What my son's comment showed was that Santa Claus can be made real by the faith of his followers.

Imagine what it would be like if Jesus dominated Christmas the way Santa does. What if all the TV specials were based on biblical texts? What if friends kept asking what Jesus will do for us this Christmas? What if it was Jesus, Jesus, Jesus all Christmas long? Why, it would almost be enough to make believers out of people!

So let Jesus be the Lord of the holidays and of every day. Worship him, talk about him, ask about him so incessantly that his living presence cannot be doubted, especially by the children.

THE CHURCH YESTERDAY

Study of church history should increase our humility about who we are and what we believe. There is nothing that the modern church enjoys that is not a gift from previous generations of God's people. . . . The more we know about how those gifts have come down to us, the more we may humbly thank God for his faithfulness to past generations, as well as to our own.

—MARK A. NOLL

Harvard philosopher George Santayana famously said, "Those who cannot remember the past are condemned to repeat it." There are good historical reasons for saying this. Certain kinds of mistakes keep cropping up in the annals of human history. To cite just one notable example, Hitler repeated Napoleon's proud blunder by attempting to invade Russia; and like Napoleon, he was completely defeated.

When it comes to mistakes, there are also good theological reasons for saying that we are prone to repeat them. Human nature has not changed. We are as susceptible to error, folly, and misjudgment as ever. This is due to our finitude (our limitations as creatures) and to our fallenness (our condition as sinful creatures). History is partly a tragic record of human depravity.

There are other lessons that we can learn by studying the past, however. Human history is also a record of God's providence. Although usually we can do no more than guess what our Father is doing, sometimes we are able to recognize his hand at work in history. As the psalmist wrote, "He brings one down, he exalts another" (Ps. 75:7b). Ultimately all of the incidents and accidents of history can be traced back to the providence of God.

God especially is at work among his people. The history of his church contains many inspiring examples of good theology and godly conduct. Past eras of the church tend to be strong where we are weak, and thus they serve to correct the besetting sins of contemporary Christianity.

The church has not met with unbroken success, however. To study its history is constantly to be confronted with pride and prejudice, schism and sin. We study church history to avoid the mistakes of the past as well as to learn from its examples. But even the mistakes often testify to the providential working of God's grace, which is able to make the best of any bad situation and to get the most out of every sinful saint. In spite of our depravity, our Father is always at work.

The following essays touch on five key events in church history—one from each of the first five centuries of the last millennium. Part of their purpose is to show the value of knowing some church history. When we see God at work in and through his people in the past, we are encouraged to believe that he is also working with us in the present.

49

AS FAR AS THE EAST
IS FROM THE WEST

1054 was the year of the Great Schism, the tragic and final split between the church in the East and the church in the West.[1]

The East and the West had always had their differences. Some of these differences were geographic and cultural. Eastern Christianity was centered on Constantinople, and the theologians of the East wrote in Greek. Western Christianity was centered on Rome, where people communicated in Latin.

There were differences in worship too. The Eastern church used icons as an aid to worship. An icon is a stylized portrait of a saint, a biblical figure, or even of Christ. Eastern worshipers venerated these icons by kissing them as they entered the church.

But the most significant difference between Eastern Orthodoxy and biblical Christianity had to do with the person of the Holy Spirit. In the expanded form of the Nicene Creed (381), Christians confessed faith "in the Holy Ghost, the Lord and Giver of life, who proceedeth from the Father." However, two centuries later, at the Synod of Toledo in 589, the church added this phrase: "We believe in the Holy Spirit, who proceeds from the Father *and the Son.*"

The Latin term used to change the creeds was *filioque,* meaning "and the Son," so this dispute is often called the "filioque controversy." Both sides agreed that the Holy Spirit is of the same substance with the Father and the Son, equal with them in power and glory. But they differed in their understanding of the relationships among the three persons of the Trinity.

Eastern theologians taught that the Spirit comes only from the Father. They were trying to safeguard his individuality, his unique identity. They were outraged that the Western church had so casually added a major doctrine to the creed. Although this happened in 589, the Eastern church has never forgiven the West for it.

What does the Bible teach? The New Testament often describes the Spirit as the "Spirit of Christ." A good example is Romans 8:9, which calls the Spirit both the "Spirit of God" and the "Spirit of Christ" (cf. Gal. 4:6). The Spirit is called the Spirit of Christ because he brings Christ to us. As Jesus promised, "He will bring glory to me by taking from what is mine and making it known to you" (John 16:14). The Spirit is the one who teaches Christ to us and enables us to trust in him.

The reason the Spirit brings Christ to us is because he was sent by the Son as well as the Father. This is what Jesus promised his disciples: "When the Counselor comes, whom I will send to you from the Father, the Spirit of truth who goes out from the Father" (John 15:26). This gives us a glimpse of the relationships within the Trinity, where the Spirit proceeds from the Father and the Son.

The dispute between East and West came to a head in 1054. The leaders of the two churches had been squabbling for control of Greek churches in Italy. The Roman pope sent a letter to Constantinople, asserting his right to "have an unfettered jurisdiction over the whole Church . . . because the [Pope] is judged by none."[2] When the patriarch of the Eastern church refused to accept this letter, the pope's representative took an order of excommunication and placed it on the altar of the great church of Hagia Sophia.

The ill will created by this rash act has lasted for a millennium. Several councils have been held to try to heal the divide between East and West (Lyons, 1274; Florence, 1438–1439; Jerusalem, 1964). But the differences between East and West continue to isolate the Eastern Orthodox Church not only from the Roman Catholic Church but also from the churches of the Reformation. For example, Orthodox adherents continue to venerate icons. But biblical Christians have always viewed this practice as a form of idolatry, the kind of worship by images that the Bible expressly forbids (Ex. 20:4).

The main lesson to be learned from the Great Schism is the danger of division in the church. Division in the church never goes away on its own. In this case, the results of careless theology and rash words have lasted for a thousand years.

Remember that division is equally dangerous at the personal level. Our petty disputes may not turn out to be as catastrophic as the Great Schism of 1054. Still, even minor breaches in our unity hinder the work and worship of the church.

If anyone has anything against us, the Scripture tells us to take the initiative to go and be reconciled (Matt. 5:24). We do this in the hope that one day the prayer of our Lord will be answered: "May they be brought to complete unity to let the world know that you sent me and have loved them even as you have loved me" (John 17:23).

56

ON A CRUSADE

*T*he Crusades began shortly before the twelfth century, and they lasted long afterwards. The crusading movement started in 1095, when Pope Urban II (1088–1099) announced that it was the will of God for Christians to deliver the Holy Land from Muslim occupation. In a series of seven Crusades spread out over the next two hundred years, European nobles, knights, squires, and foot soldiers tried to capture the land where Christ was born, died, and rose again.

It is hard to think of anything good to say about the Crusades. Church history has many sordid episodes, but the Crusades marked perhaps the lowest point of all. They took place, after all, during the Dark Ages.

There were two major problems with the Crusades. One was the goal. Aside from the political aspirations of the pope, the Crusades were intended to reopen Jerusalem for Christian pilgrimages. Yet the recapture of Palestine served little spiritual purpose.

True, there is great value in visiting the Bible lands. Every Christian should try to visit Israel at least once during his or her lifetime. The Christian faith rests upon historical events that took place in real physical locations. Many biblical truths take on new significance when one has firsthand knowledge of biblical archaeology and geography—the kind of knowledge that can only come from making a personal visit.

Yet there is nothing intrinsically holy about the so-called holy sites of the so-called Holy Land. The kind of worshipers God seeks are those who worship him "in spirit and in truth" (John 4:24), not the kind who consider one place more sacred than another.

Treating Palestine as holy ground tends to bring out the worst forms of religion. One thinks of the transparent platform built just under the surface of the Sea of Galilee so people can walk on water. Or of Pope John Paul II granting indulgences to Roman Catholics who made a pilgrimage to Israel in the year 2000.[1] Or of the garish shrines that dot Israel's landscape, in many cases obscuring the original landscape. These forms of externalism all come from the tendency to worship things and places rather than the living God.

As unnecessary as their objective was, the method the Crusaders used to achieve it was even worse. The Crusades were known as holy wars, but they were anything but. In fact, they were unspeakably brutal. Already by 1099 the Crusaders had succeeded in capturing Jerusalem, but their victory came at the cost of many Muslim, Jewish, and Christian lives.

It is always a mistake for the church to wage conventional warfare. We do better to remember the words Jesus spoke when his companions tried to defend him with a stroke of the sword: "Put your sword back in its place," Jesus said to him, "for all who draw the sword will die by the sword" (Matt. 26:52). The only weapons the church has in its arsenal are spiritual weapons like faith, prayer, and the Word of God. If the church fights with anything else, then it is using the wrong means, and probably pursuing the wrong ends as well. The Crusaders failed on both counts: they used ungodly means to pursue an unworthy goal.

The worst atrocity of the Crusades was the sack of Byzantium (1204), where the Crusaders stopped for three days of destruction on their way to Palestine. According to one historian, they

> were filled with a lust for destruction. They rushed in a howling mob down the streets and through the houses, snatching up every-thing that glittered and destroying whatever they could not carry, pausing only to murder or to rape. . . . Wounded women and chil-dren lay dying in the streets. For three days the ghastly scenes of pillage and bloodshed continued, till the huge and beautiful city was a shambles.[2]

Since Byzantium was the home of the Eastern church, its destruction only reinforced the breach between East and West.

The brutality of the Crusades also created bitter animosity between Christians and Muslims. To this day, the Crusades are an open wound in the Islamic world, for which the church is held responsible. Muslims will never forget that so-called Christianity did its worst to disturb the peace of the Middle East. It is little wonder that to this day a vast number of Mus-lims remain hostile to the Gospel. In many ways Islamic *jihad* is the logical consequence of the Crusades.

In the year 2000, a group of Christians decided to do something to undo the damage caused by the Crusades. They traveled from Europe to Asia Minor, retracing the steps of the first Crusaders on their way to the city of Jerusalem. Along the way they stopped at various sites along the tra-ditional route to Jerusalem, trying to visit as many mosques as they could. In each city they sought forgiveness from the Muslim community for the sins of the medieval church.

It was a case of better late than never. The church never should have tried to capture Jerusalem, especially the way it tried to do it. The least we can do now is lament for the sins of the past and pray that God might yet pour out his grace on the Muslim world. The Crusades serve as a permanent reminder to Christians not to be overconfident that we know what God wills or overzealous in trying to achieve our interpretation of his will by force.

51

WHEN CATHOLICS
WERE CATHOLIC

*O*ne good reason to take a backward glance at the last millennium is
to remind ourselves that church history did not begin with the
Protestant Reformation in Europe. By the providence of God, the Reformation rediscovered the Gospel for our times. But people were repenting
of their sins and trusting in Jesus Christ for their salvation centuries before
Martin Luther posted his ninety-five theses on the door of the Wittenburg
church.

There was a time when people who belonged to the church belonged
to the church in Rome and when people who belonged to the church in
Rome belonged to the one true church. To put it another way, there was a

time when Catholics were catholic. "Catholic" means "universal." For example, when Christians recite the Apostles' Creed, we say we believe in the "holy catholic church," which means that there is only one worldwide church of Jesus Christ. Properly speaking, the real catholic church consists of all believers in Jesus Christ. And there was a time when (even) Catholics were catholic.

The church was like that in the thirteenth century, a century most Protestants have long since forgotten. Too easily we move from Augustine of Hippo in the fifth century to Martin Luther in the sixteenth century, carelessly skipping over the intervening millennium. The eleventh century is barely remembered for the schism between East and West. The twelfth century had its infamous Crusades. But the thirteenth century, at the tired end of the Dark Ages, is almost entirely forgotten.

The great theologian of the thirteenth century was Thomas Aquinas (c. 1225–1274). Aquinas is usually considered a Roman Catholic theologian, and he was, but he is our theologian too, because he lived when Catholics were catholic.

Aquinas was an accomplished philosopher, famous for his proofs for the existence of God. He also wrote many commentaries and theological treatises, the greatest of which was his monumental *Summa Theologiae*, a complete systematic theology. Many parts of his theology were thoroughly biblical. Aquinas believed and taught fundamental doctrines like the Trinity, creation, sin, the deity of Jesus Christ, predestination, and so forth.

In his own way, Aquinas even believed that the chief end of man is to glorify God and enjoy him forever. He said, "Among all the goals of human actions one is ultimate. . . . Men attain their goal by coming to know God and love him. . . . We call man's way of attaining his goal being happy."[1] Being happy may sound overly self-centered. But Aquinas went on to explain that what makes human beings happiest of all is to contemplate God and all his perfections.

Obviously Thomas Aquinas can still be read with profit, as can many other theologians who wrote prior to the Reformation. Yet reading his

Summa also shows why the Reformation was necessary. For one thing, it contains many of the standard Roman Catholic errors, such as unbiblical views of Mary, unwarranted additions to the sacraments, and improper elevations of papal authority to the level of Holy Scripture. But the main reason the church needed to be reformed was because the medieval church had practically lost sight of the grace of God in salvation.

The writings of Thomas Aquinas give a good indication of what Christians were starting to believe and teach about faith and works in the thirteenth century. They were starting to believe, for example, that grace works with us so that we can win our way to heaven. In the words of Aquinas, "Our actions earn the good God has planned as man's reward."[2] He was quick to say that salvation first comes by a free gift. "But," he went on to say, "once one has grace—to begin good works—one can earn further grace as a result of those works."[3]

This is why it is never enough to say that justification comes by faith, which is what orthodox Roman Catholics say to this day. This is not enough because the only justification God offers comes by faith *alone*. No doubt the apostle Paul would pose the same question to Aquinas that he posed to the Galatians: "After beginning with the Spirit, are you now trying to attain your goal by human effort?" (Gal. 3:3). Like the Galatians, although Aquinas and other medieval theologians started with faith, they continued by works.

This shows why the Reformation was necessary. Aquinas may well have been a genuine believer. He probably was. Thankfully, one does not have to be able to explain the doctrine of justification by faith alone in order to be saved by it. One has only to believe in Jesus Christ. But by the thirteenth century, the true message of salvation was getting obscured and it was in danger of being lost altogether.

The example of Thomas Aquinas also reminds us to continue to pray for the saving work of the Holy Spirit within the Roman Catholic Church. Sometimes we forget that Luther, Calvin, and the rest of the Reformers were born and bred within the Roman church. When Catholics were catholic, they were Catholic too, and it was within the Roman church that they came to saving faith in Jesus Christ.

To be sure, the pope would not tolerate their plain teaching of the gospel, so eventually they were thrown out of the church. But God can and does carry out his saving work to this day, even where his gospel is not preached in all its clarity.

Toward that end, we should pray for the recovery of the gospel and the salvation of sinners within the Roman Catholic Church. In the year 2000 the Archdiocese of Philadelphia worked hard to get its parishioners back to church. More than one million Roman Catholics in the Philadelphia area received mailings and heard radio ads inviting them to come back to the Mother Church and do penance. It is a good thing to go back to church, but all the better when the church preaches the one true gospel. We should continue to pray accordingly.

52

WYCLIFFE, BIBLE
TRANSLATOR

I am sometimes asked which translation of the Bible I recommend.
There are dozens of versions to choose from. The old standard is still
the King James Version (KJV), first printed in 1611. These days Tenth
Presbyterian Church uses the New International Version (NIV), which is
more casual in its text and translation but also easier to understand. There
are loads of other options: the Revised Standard Version (RSV), the New
American Standard Bible (NASB), the New English Bible (NEB), the New
Living Translation (NLT), and the one that is becoming my favorite: the
English Standard Version (ESV).

I use different translations for different reasons. The New International Version (NIV) is not my favorite, but it has become the standard version for many evangelical churches. There are certain advantages to the church sharing a common Bible. The New King James Version (NKJV) is better to read aloud because it retains many of the elegant rhythms of the old King James. With my children I sometimes use the New Living Translation (NLT), although sometimes I wonder how much easier it really is to understand. The New American Standard Bible (NASB) is good to consult to get a feel for the Greek or Hebrew original. But whichever translation I use—and this is the important thing—I am confident of its basic reliability. Anyone who uses any of the standard English Bible translations is reading the authoritative Word of God.

There are some problems with having so many translations available. One problem is memory work. For Christians who are familiar with more than one translation, it can be hard to remember the exact wording of a verse. As a child, I did most of my memory work in the King James Version. Now I find that I need to keep a King James concordance handy whenever I am looking for a verse, because I can't always find it in the NIV. Also, some families have difficulty because they have learned the same verse in two or three different versions. We have lost a common Bible, a Bible everyone knows by ear and by heart.

Christians did not have that problem in the fourteenth century. Instead of having the luxury of a dozen translations to choose from, the Bible was not available in English at all.

The man who began to rectify the situation was John Wycliffe (c. 1330–1384), the Bible translator. Wycliffe had always recognized the authority of the Scriptures of the Old and New Testaments. For his doctoral work at the University of Oxford he took the unusual step of producing a short commentary on the whole Bible. Rather than spending his time studying what philosophers and theologians were saying about the Bible, he wanted to study the Bible in its original languages.

Wycliffe's study of the Bible eventually led him into direct conflict with the Roman Catholic Church, which in those days took a dim view of lay people studying the Bible. Wycliffe argued that the church was wrong to add its doctrines to those taught in Holy Scripture. He believed that the Bible, and the Bible alone, is the only standard in matters of Christian theology and practice. Thus he heeded the biblical proverb: "Every word of God is flawless. . . . Do not add to his words, or he will rebuke you and prove you a liar" (Prov. 30:5–6).

Wycliffe's study of the Bible eventually led him into other areas of disagreement with the church in Rome. He denied that the Scripture gave any doctrinal authority to the pope. He doubted whether there was any biblical precedent for monasteries. He opposed the Catholic idea that Christ is physically present in the sacrament of the Lord's Supper. Wycliffe preached boldly on all these matters. He also taught the necessity of having personal faith in Jesus Christ, which means that he believed two major Reformation doctrines even before there was a Reformation: *sola Scriptura* (the Bible alone) and *sola fide* (by faith alone).

What Wycliffe chiefly is remembered for, however, is making the Bible available in English. It is hard to explain why the church resisted translating the Bible for so long. The Catholics did finally issue portions of the Bible in English in 1582. Yet they doubted whether it was necessary to put the Bible into words people could understand. In their preface they wrote, "Yet we must not imagine that in the primitive Church . . . the translated Bibles into the vulgar tongues, were in the hands of every husbandman, artificer, prentice, boys, girls, mistress, maid, man. . . . No, in those better times men were neither so ill, nor so curious of themselves, so to abuse the blessed book of Christ."[1] In other words, ordinary folks can't be trusted to read the Bible for themselves!

Wycliffe knew better, which is why he did much of his preaching in English. Inspired by his example, his followers produced an English version of the Old Testament during the 1380s. A number of copies of that manuscript were made, but it would take more than a century until the whole Bible was printed in English.

The reason for the delay is not hard to find. According to the Catholic

Constitutions of Oxford (1408), no one was allowed to translate the Bible into English, upon pain of death. That order was not defied until William Tyndale (c. 1494–1536) finally published his English New Testament in 1526. Tyndale was burned at the stake, but the work of Bible translation could not be stopped. Miles Coverdale produced an edition of the entire Bible in 1535, and a number of other translations were made before King James authorized the version published in 1611.

Today there are many Bibles available in English. Maybe too many. But there was a time when there were no versions at all. Anyone who reads the Bible in English owes John Wycliffe a debt of gratitude, for he was the first to give us the Word of God in a language we can understand.

53

BONFIRE OF THE VANITIES

*M*ore than five hundred years ago, on May 23, 1498, Savonarola was burned at the stake.[1] The citizens of Florence mourned, and the poets lamented his passing:

> Charity is extinct,
> Love of God is no more.
> All are lukewarm;
> And without living faith. . . .
> Alas! the Saint is dead!
> Alas! O Lord! Alas!

Thou hast taken our Prophet
And drawn him to thyself.

Girolamo Savonarola (1452–1498), the great Italian preacher, was one of the forerunners of the Protestant Reformation. He is worthy of our consideration because his life and death illustrate the problems the church was facing in the fifteenth century.

Savonarola was born and reared within the Roman Catholic church. As a young man he decided to go into the ministry and he became a friar in a Dominican monastery. Before long it was apparent that he was a gifted Bible scholar, and at the age of thirty he was sent to Florence, where his primary duty was the exposition of Scripture.

As a preacher traveling throughout the city and the surrounding countryside, Savonarola began to attack the widespread corruption in Italian culture and the Roman Catholic Church. Gradually his sermons attracted the attention of the leading politicians and intellectuals of the day, men like Lorenzo de' Medici, the ruler of Florence, and the philosopher Pico della Mirandola.

Savonarola's preaching had a prophetic tone. He predicted that the city of Florence would have to endure a period of intense suffering before it could be restored and reformed. The only way divine judgment could be averted was if the people repented of their sins, sought to be united to Christ by faith, and began to imitate his perfect life of loving obedience.

When the French army invaded Italy in 1494, Savonarola's prophecies seemed to be fulfilled. Florence became enemy-occupied territory. But this led to the restoration of the city, in part through Savonarola's efforts. He persuaded the French king not to destroy the city, and he helped to reorganize its government as a republic.

Savonarola became about as popular as it is possible for a preacher to become. He was able to use his influence to create a welfare system to care for the poor and the sick. He also did everything he could to encourage education, science, and the arts. His goal was to establish a new culture based on biblical principles rather than humanistic ones.

Savonarola did not stop preaching, however, and he continued to speak out against sexual immorality, prostitution, gambling, blasphemy, drunkenness, and other common sins. He helped start prayer meetings on the city streets and staged public conflagrations at which people burned pornography, gambling equipment, and even cosmetics. These "bonfires of the vanities," as they were called, were intended to help purge the city of evil.

Sooner or later, preachers who teach and apply the Bible are bound to run into opposition, especially if they preach against the sins that people enjoy. Savonarola was no exception. Eventually his scathing comments about the church got him into trouble. He had come to doubt whether it was biblical for the ministry of the church to be based around convents and monasteries, at least the way they were run at that time. He also began to attack the excessive luxury of the pope and his court.

Word of Savonarola's preaching eventually reached the Vatican, and in 1495 Pope Alexander VI summoned him to Rome to defend his ministry. Although he was still Catholic in his doctrine, Savonarola refused to go to Rome, in part because he believed that the pope was a servant of Satan rather than a follower of Christ.

He continued preaching in Florence for several more years. As a result of his defiance, eventually he was excommunicated, arrested, tortured, hanged, and burned. Before Savonarola died, he uttered this famous lament for his adopted city: "Thy sins, O Florence, are the cause of these stripes. But now repent, offer prayers, become united. I have wearied myself all the days of my life to make known to thee the truths of the faith, and of holy living; and I have had nothing but tribulations, derision, and reproach."[2]

Savonarola is a good example to follow. His life and death confirm Paul's words to Timothy: "Everyone who wants to live a godly life in Christ Jesus will be persecuted, while evil men and impostors will go from bad to worse, deceiving and being deceived. But as for you, continue in what you have learned" (2 Tim. 3:12–14a).

We need to continue in what we have learned because we face many of the same issues Savonarola faced. Gambling and sexual sin are rampant.

Many of the leading artists and politicians of our day follow secular principles rather than biblical ones. And the evangelical church is part of the problem. The behavior of those who call themselves Christians is often hard to distinguish from those who do not. If the ads in evangelical magazines and the ecclesiastical junk mail are any indication, many churches are more interested in material prosperity than spiritual vitality.

How little has changed in the last five hundred years! Savonarola witnessed the same kinds of corruption in his day that we witness in ours. Ultimately he despaired of being able to do much about it. Perhaps the only thing he failed to see clearly was the doctrine that best reforms the church: the doctrine of justification by faith alone.

Savonarola was not a Protestant. Yet his preaching on spiritual renewal helped prepare the way for a sort of Italian Reformation. And in the middle of the next century, when Pope Paul IV examined Savonarola's writings, he said, "This is Martin Luther, this doctrine is pestiferous!"[3]

THE CHURCH TODAY

Winning back members of the Body of Christ will not be done by imitating the techniques of the culture industries. Those who can be ransomed will be drawn to a radically reformed and revitalized vision of the Church and its role in Jesus' mission—or they will not be ransomed at all.

—MICHAEL BUDDE

This book has been about Christians in the world. What does it mean to be in the world but not of the world? How can we resist harmful non-Christian attitudes about singleness and the family? What is the Christian perspective on science and the arts? How should Christians respond to the pressing social issues of the day?

Instead of relating Christianity to the world, the essays in this last section primarily deal with what is happening in the church. What does Christianity have to offer? What does the church teach about sin and judgment? What is God doing in the Christian community? What does it mean to be a church for the twenty-first century?

We often hear Christian leaders say that we are living in a new spiritual context, one that requires a new way of "doing church." It is true that the world around us is changing. This is always the case. The church constantly faces new challenges from the surrounding culture. This is why it is always important for Christians to notice what is happening in the world and to think about it from the biblical point of view. The essays in this book are part of an ongoing enterprise to understand and interpret what is happening in our Father's world.

One reason it is important to think Christianly about culture is that what happens in the world has a way of coming into the church. As our culture becomes increasingly secular, the church becomes increasingly secular too. Postmodern times almost inevitably produce a postmodern church.

Do these cultural changes mean that we need to develop a whole new pattern for church life? On the contrary, the more things change, the more some things need to stay the same. It is more important than ever to maintain the biblical pattern for life in our Father's house.

We still believe in prayer and the preaching of God's Word. We believe in the power of the gospel to change people's lives. We believe in worshiping God in the biblical way, including the proper administration of the sacraments. We believe in loving God and loving our neighbors. We believe in keeping the fellowship of the Holy Spirit. And we believe that even today God is doing something important in the church.

54

CONSUMER REPORT ON RELIGION

"What Religion Is the Best Religion?" That was the question at the top of a Web page sponsored by the online magazine *Fade to Black*. "Religion has been with man for thousands of years," the editors said, "but with so many to choose from how do you know which one is right for you?"

It was a good question—in a way, the most important question there is. To get some answers, *Fade to Black* staged an experiment. They asked a team of nearly forty independent volunteers to try the following major world religions: Catholicism, Christianity, Buddhism, Islam, and Judaism, as well as atheism, Hinduism, and Satanism. The volunteers, who were aborigines from the Brazilian rain forest, were given four weeks to test each of the alternatives. Eight months later, they scored the religions in four categories: ritual—the fewer rituals the better; sin threshold—how much can you get away with before you have to repent?; penalty for sin—what price do you have to pay when you do sin?; and ease of getting into heaven—how much work does it take to reach the state of perfect bliss?

Which religion came out on top? Would you believe that it was Christianity? The testers scored Christianity higher than nearly every other religion in nearly every category, which led the researchers to conclude, "If you are looking for a good over-all religion, you can't go wrong with Christianity. It ranked the highest among the tribesmen and very high in our scholarly test." Catholicism ranked a close second, while atheism came in dead last.

The consumer report on religion is a spoof, a mock investigation, as is evident from the humorous comments scattered throughout. Yet it provides an interesting commentary on popular attitudes about religion in general and about Christianity in particular.

All joking aside, the report seems to understand some basic theological principles. First, it recognizes that in one way or another, religion is supposed to help us deal with the problem of sin. Because we live in a moral universe, there is a real difference between right and wrong, and somehow our wrongs have to be paid for. The problem that any religion must solve is the problem of sin. The report also generally affirms the possibility of a life to come. The best thing that any religion can offer is the hope of heaven, the promise of eternal life.

Somewhat surprisingly, the report recognizes the inherent problem with works righteousness. Any religion that depends on what *we* have to do is too difficult. "If you prefer a lot of rules and customs," the editors say, "take a look into Judaism, or the Muslim religions." But for that reason, Judaism and Islam scored poorly in the test. Christianity was preferred because it offers salvation as a free gift, which is what the Bible teaches: "For it is by grace you have been saved, through faith—and this not from yourselves, it is the gift of God—not by works, so that no one can boast" (Eph. 2:8–9).

The fact that Christianity came out on top sounds encouraging until one examines the criteria. The standard for determining the best religion was selfish. The testers were looking for a religion that required less work and offered more freedom to, as they put it, "do as you please without re-penting." This is what most people are looking for: a religion that offers the greatest reward at the least cost.

In some ways, Christianity *is* the easiest religion. It has few rituals, and the rituals that it does have—such as baptism, for example, or the Lord's Supper—tend to be simple. There are no dietary laws to keep, no pilgrim-ages to make, and no penance to perform. Christianity also offers the easi-est pathway to heaven. Although the consumer report didn't go into many details, all that is required is faith in Jesus Christ. He is the way and the truth and the life (John 14:6).

But of all the reasons to become a Christian, the idea that it will be easy is one of the most misleading, because Christianity isn't easy at all. What makes it seem easy is that Jesus Christ does all the hard work. Salvation is a free gift offered on the basis of his sufferings and death. However, for many Christians, coming to Christ proves to be one of the hardest things they ever do. This is because trusting in Christ means to stop trusting in one's self, which is what most people are most unwilling to do.

When people stop trusting in themselves and start trusting in Christ, they usually find that the Christian life is full of sacrifice and difficulty. Je-sus demands that his followers give up everything to follow him. Often he gives us most of our lives back, in a new and wonderful way. But in princi-ple the Christian must give up everything. As Dietrich Bonhoeffer said, "When Christ calls a man, he bids him come and die."[1] But we are afraid to die, even if the only death required is death to self.

It is important not to give non-Christians the impression that the Christian life is easy. In sharing our faith, both of these truths must be kept in mind: First, salvation is a free gift of God's grace. All that anyone has to do is trust in Jesus Christ. Second, becoming a Christian will cost us every-thing we have. To follow Christ is to give up the right to run our own lives. It is to surrender control over our time and our money, our work and our leisure, our family and friends—everything. While there are many good reasons to become a Christian, the idea that it is easy to follow Christ is not one of them!

55

A SHORT THEOLOGY
OF THE TULIP

*T*he Rykens try to grow tulips every spring. It has become an annual act of piety for us, in part because it is a family tradition. My Dutch grandfather used to help plant a hundred thousand bulbs every year in preparation for Tulip Time in Pella, Iowa. He had to dig them back up again, too, and store them over the winter.

Every fall we plant tulip bulbs in our city window boxes, carefully spacing them out and pushing them down to the right depth of the soil. Add a little bone meal, and the tulips are ready for the long, cold winter. For months we wait for them, longing for spring, lovingly taking the boxes down to the garage when there is a hard freeze.

Finally spring arrives. The first tulips appear, a blade here and a blade there, tentatively searching for a warm ray of sunlight. Almost overnight, the boxes are filled with short, straight shoots, like so many sticks of dynamite, ready to explode into color. We wait for what the Irish poet Dylan Thomas called "the force that through the green fuse drives the flower."

What is the theological significance of growing tulips? All of life is lived unto God. If I am going to plant tulips, I need to know how tulips glorify God. What do they reveal about the mind of their Maker?

To begin with, tulips testify to God's love of beauty and to the immense variety of his creativity. The *International Register* produced annually by the Royal General Bulbgrowers' Association in the Netherlands lists nearly six thousand varieties of tulip. There have been some great tulips in history as well: the red and white streaks of the famous Semper Augustus, the striking yellow and black of Lawrence's Polyphemus, and so on.

The many varieties of tulip also testify to the creativity of human beings, for many hybrids have been cultivated by amateur florists. By carefully breeding special varieties, tulip lovers have allowed the possibilities of the God-given tulip to blossom.

The Bible does not mention tulips specifically. However, biblical scholars tell us that the phrase "lilies of the field" refers to many different kinds of flowers, including the tulip.[1] So when Jesus said that the lilies of the field have more splendor than Solomon (Matt. 6:28–29), he was talking about tulips, among other kinds of flowers.

What the Bible says about flowers is rather surprising. It does not praise their beauty, primarily. Instead, it shows how transient that beauty is, often comparing it to the fading glory of human beings. In the words of Isaiah,

> All men are like grass,
>> and all their glory is like the flowers of the field.
> The grass withers and the flowers fall,
>> because the breath of the LORD blows on them.
>> (Isa. 40:6–7; cf. Ps. 103:15–16)

Similarly, Job said, "[Man] springs up like a flower and withers away" (Job 14:2).

After what happened to our tulips one spring, we Rykens know what the Bible is talking about. That year was a major disappointment in the tulip department. Our flowers were short, for one thing, although we felt better about that once we realized they were a dwarf variety. But they lived for only a week before they began to wilt. The grass withers. The flowers fade. And those of us who are casual gardeners are reminded that our labor is under God's curse (Gen. 3:17–19).

But tulips in springtime are also a sign of God's grace. Every year we place dozens of them on the platform at Tenth Church to help us celebrate the Philadelphia Conference on Reformation Theology. Every theological system should have its own flower, and the official flower of Reformation theology is the tulip. The Arminians have their daisies, in keeping with their "he loves me, he loves me not" approach to eternal security. But Reformation Christians have always been partial to tulips, especially during times of religious persecution. The Huguenots brought tulips when they fled from France to England in the late seventeenth century. In the 1800s my Dutch ancestors brought tulips from the Netherlands to America.

One reason the tulip is the official flower for Reformation theology is because the word *tulip* is an acronym for some of its major doctrines:

T stands for "total depravity." We are all sinners all the way through (Gen. 6:5; Rom. 3:23).

U stands for "unconditional election." God chose to save us for reasons known only to him (Eph. 1:4–5).

L stands for "limited atonement." Christ got what he paid for when he died for his people, and his people alone (John 10:14–15).

I stands for "irresistible grace." When the Spirit changes our hearts, we will and we must come to God in faith (John 6:44–45).

P stands for the "perseverance of the saints." Our faithful God will see us safely to our eternal home (Rom. 8:28, 30).

What makes that acronym especially appropriate is that those theological principles were fully explained at the Synod of Dort (1616–1619), which was held in the Netherlands. Thus, for almost four hundred years, both the best tulips and the soundest theology have come from Holland!

Tulips should remind us of human depravity, and when it comes to depravity, Calvinists not only believe in it, we practice it! This can be well illustrated from the history of the tulip. In the 1630s, tulipomania swept the Netherlands.[2] Defying all sanity, tulip bulbs became the hottest-selling item in the country.

As buyers bid wildly for scarce bulbs, the tulip became the ultimate status symbol. At one auction, the contemporary equivalent of ten million dollars changed hands, and a single bulb of the Admiral van Enkhuijsen sold for 5,400 guilders, or fifteen years' wages, more than the price for a townhouse in the best quarter of Amsterdam. Then, as suddenly as the craze began, it ended. The tulip market crashed, fortunes were lost, and speculators went bankrupt—thus proving the folly of their greed.

But the tulip should remind us of something more than our depravity. Its beauty should also remind us that from beginning to end, salvation is all of God. It is by his grace alone that we are saved: his grace to choose, his grace to atone, his grace to regenerate, and his grace to bring us home.

56

THE PLACE OF HELL

*N*ot long after I entered the pastorate, I was quoted at some length in a *Philadelphia Inquirer* article entitled "Anglican's Take on the Netherworld Stirs Fiery Debate."[1] A few days before, I had received a note in my church mailbox, saying that the paper had telephoned for Dr. James Montgomery Boice, our senior minister. Since Dr. Boice was out of town, the religion editor wondered if I would be interested in granting an interview on the doctrine of hell! I was interested, of course, although I also had some feelings of trepidation.

On the one hand, ministers are always available to speak to the religious issues of our day. That is part of our calling: to proclaim the Word of God. On the other hand, there were plenty of other topics I would have preferred to discuss. When the media want to cover religion, they generally don't want to know what they must do to be saved. Instead, they want to know whether demons really carry pitchforks. Furthermore, to give an interview is to put oneself at the mercy of the interviewer. Even if a journalist is not hostile toward biblical Christianity, it is easy for things to be misquoted or taken out of context in such a way that dishonor is brought to the church of Jesus Christ. With that in mind, we quickly mobilized members of the church staff and others to pray for both the interview and the upcoming article.

On Sunday morning before church, one of my colleagues cheerfully telephoned to say that my name was all over the papers. I didn't have a chance to see a copy, however, so I spent the rest of the morning worrying about having said something stupid or controversial. My fears were laid to rest when the elders met for prayer and Dr. Boice triumphantly said, "The Anglicans abolished hell, but Phil Ryken reinstated it!"

What prompted the article was the decision by a commission of the Church of England to abandon the orthodox doctrine of hell. They concluded: "Hell is not eternal torment, but it is the final and irrevocable choosing of that which is opposed to God so completely and so absolutely that the only end is total non-being."

The Anglican pronouncement was not surprising. What one scholar has called *The Decline of Hell* was already a notable feature of Anglican theology in the seventeenth century.[2] Even in evangelical circles in England, hell was on the defensive in the twentieth century. The doctrine commission was ratifying what many Anglican clergy and parishioners already believed—or didn't believe—about hell.

What is more important than the place of hell in the Church of England is the place of hell in the Bible. Is hell nothing more than nonexistence? That is what many people would like to believe. They wouldn't mind being blotted out of existence. But that's not what the Bible teaches. The Bible describes hell as a place of darkness, misery, conscious anguish, and fire. To be in hell is to be separated from the presence, grace, and compassion of God. There is no need to speculate about what else might be included in hell or to add to its miseries. It is enough to know that hell is a horrible place (see Matt. 5:22; 25:31–46; Luke 16:19–31; Rev. 20:10–15).

The most striking feature of the doctrine of hell is that the biggest proportion of what the Bible has to say about hell is found in the gospels. The chief proponent of the doctrine of hell is Jesus Christ. He is the one who said, "Depart from me, you who are cursed, into the eternal fire prepared for the devil and his angels" (Matt. 25:41). And he is the one who said, "They will go away to eternal punishment, but the righteous to eternal life" (Matt. 25:46).

Hell is a topic that most people want to avoid. When hell is mentioned, most people either joke about it or say something like, "That sounds awful; let's not talk about it." Secular people don't want to talk about it because they have enough of a guilty conscience to suspect that if there is a hell, they probably belong in it. Christians don't want to talk about it because they have plenty of friends who don't know Christ but seem nice enough not to deserve eternal punishment.

If it's true that most people don't want to think about hell, then why did Jesus talk about it? It must have been because he did not want his disciples to be ignorant about the subject. If hell is a place, then the last thing Jesus would do is pretend that it doesn't exist. Instead, he would teach his disciples the truth about hell in the most explicit terms. And that is what he did. Jesus taught that sin is so evil in the sight of a holy God that it deserves eternal punishment. At the same time, he endured the judgment of God against sin in his body, so that anyone who comes to him in faith and repentance does not have to endure hell. Jesus gave his disciples a clear view of hell so that they would have a clear view of salvation.

In this respect, as in all others, a minister should follow the example of his Lord. One of the things I was interviewed about that didn't make it into the paper was the place of hell in our preaching. I pointed out that evangelicals preach about hell much less often than they used to. That is partly because some earlier generations preached about hell altogether more often than they should have. What we ought to do with the doctrine of hell is what we do with virtually every other doctrine found in Scripture: preach it about as often as it comes up in the Bible. In the case of hell, that's not all that often, but often enough to remind us how much God hates sin and how crucial it is to trust in Jesus Christ for salvation. This is one of the great advantages of expository preaching: it gives us the theological and practical diet the Lord intends for us to have.

There is one other thing worth saying about hell, something it would have been worth saying to the *Philadelphia Inquirer*. Hell is not humorous. Hell has a place in serious discussions about eternity, but it shouldn't have much of a place in joking around. One sign that our culture has a guilty conscience is the frequency with which hell is used in either profanity or comedy in America.

The *Inquirer* article began by mentioning that there is a place called Hell, Michigan, where visitors can buy T-shirts that read, "I've been to Hell and back." The piece ended like this: "OK. Maybe hell is a place of torment. Maybe it's a non-place of annihilation. One thing seems certain. You probably can't buy funny T-shirts there."

No, I suppose you can't. But since hell is a real place, that is hardly a laughing matter.

57

THE COMING REVIVAL

There is more and more talk these days about revival coming to America, perhaps more talk now than at any time in the past half century. There are rumors of revival. From time to time we are told that revival has come to Toronto, or to Florida, or to Chicago. There are also books about revival. Bill Bright, the founder and president of Campus Crusade for Christ, has written one called *The Coming Revival*.[1] Dale Schlafer of Promise Keepers has written *A Revival Primer* to help get us ready for it when it does come.[2] There are also conferences about revival. The Presbyterian Church in America sponsors an annual Convocation on Revival and Reformation. Its purpose is to "encourage and prepare ministers to lead their churches toward Revival and Reformation." So there is plenty of talk about revival. Is revival coming?

Before we can answer that question, we need to know what revival is. The term *revival* is biblical. It appears in prayers from the Psalms:

> Revive us, and we will call on your name.
> Restore us, O LORD God Almighty;
>> make your face shine upon us,
>> that we may be saved. (Ps. 80:18–19)

> Restore us again, O God our Savior,
>> and put away your displeasure toward us. . . .
> Will you not revive us again,
>> that your people may rejoice in you? (Ps. 85:4, 6)

Revival restores spiritual passion to God's people. Stephen Olford describes it as "that strange and sovereign work of God in which he visits his own people, restoring, reanimating, and releasing them into the fullness of His blessings."[3]

The primary cause of revival is the presence of God's Holy Spirit in great power. Martyn Lloyd-Jones (1898–1981) thus called it "a visitation of the Holy Spirit."[4] The result of that visitation is repentance for sin, which Schlafer describes like this:

> Suddenly, without warning, God is present, and the people are brought face to face with God's holiness and their sin. It seems that God is dealing with them alone so that whatever the spiritual state of the person, saved or unsaved, a mighty work of transformation occurs. The unsaved are brought to salvation, and the saved are brought to further holiness.[5]

This is the kind of revival that took place in Jerusalem when Ezra threw himself down in front of the temple and wept for the sins of God's people (Ezra 10:1). As a result of his confession, God's people repented of their sins and renewed their covenant with God (Ezra 10:2–3).

To summarize, revival is a sovereign visitation of God's Holy Spirit that brings deep repentance for sin and a renewed passion for God to the church. It is not the same thing as reformation, although revival sometimes leads to reformation. Reformation is something God brings to a culture, whereas revival is something God brings primarily to his church. It is only later that genuine, biblical Christianity begins to reshape the culture.

With that definition in mind, it is obvious that much that goes by the name *revival* these days is not revival in the biblical sense. Almost anything advertised as a revival meeting is unlikely to be a true revival. The Holy Spirit does not need a marketing department, and usually he shows up unannounced. Nor is revival guaranteed by the presence of signs and wonders—holy laughter, people falling over, and all the rest of it. The Bible warns Christians that even the devil is capable of performing outward signs and wonders (2 Thess. 2:9). The only unmistakable sign of genuine revival is repentance for sin, followed by renewed commitment to biblical Christianity.

Consider the revival that took place on the day of Pentecost. As soon as the Holy Spirit came on the early church in great power, the apostles began to preach the good news about Jesus Christ from the Scriptures (Acts 2:4, 14–39). Thus the first thing to expect when the Holy Spirit comes in power is a long, long sermon about Jesus! If a church claims to have revival without the plain teaching of the Bible, the Holy Spirit is not involved, for God's Spirit does not want to call attention to himself but to focus attention on God's Son through God's Word (see 1 Cor. 2).

There is one other potential danger in all the recent talk about revival, and that is the focus on the revival itself. People who have experienced genuine revival do not say that revival came. What they say is that God came. Since God is the reviver, there is no authentic revival without his living and powerful presence through the Holy Spirit. When God does come in power, what people talk about is not revival but God.

There is a wonderful account of the revival that took place in Britain during the 1950s, on the Isle of Lewis. It comes from the man who preached during that revival, the Reverend Duncan Campbell. The title Campbell gave to his story is significant: "When God Stepped Down from Heaven."

Since we do not know when God will step down from heaven, we cannot say whether revival is coming or not. The Holy Spirit is always present when God's people worship in the name of Jesus Christ. But we do not know when God will visit his people in the fullness of his power. We can only say that we long for God to come in power and, that in the meantime, we will commit ourselves to pray that he will.

58

PRAYING FOR REVIVAL

*I*n the preceding chapter we defined revival as a sovereign visitation of God's Holy Spirit that brings deep repentance for sin and a renewed passion for God to the church. "A revival," wrote the nineteenth-century minister Calvin Colton, "is a special and manifest outpouring of the Spirit of God when the work no longer labors in the hands of men but seems to be taken up by God himself."[1]

We concluded that despite all the recent talk about the coming revival, we cannot know for certain when revival will come. Revival comes when God comes, and who can say when the Holy Spirit will visit the church in the fullness of his power?

The only thing we can say for certain is that we long to see the Spirit revive the church in our day, as he has in times past. Asa Nettleton (1783–1844) was a preacher during the Second Great Awakening (c. 1787–1825), and he left an eyewitness account of a meeting where revival took place. He wrote:

> Did you ever witness two hundred sinners with one accord in one place weeping? The scene is beyond description. . . . I felt as though I was standing on the verge of the eternal world; while the floor under my feet was shaken by the trembling of anxious souls in view of the judgment to come.[2]

Or consider the Praying Revival of the late 1850s. That revival began with a lunchtime prayer meeting in New York City. The first week, six people came. The next week, twenty turned out. Six months later, ten thousand businessmen were meeting for prayer! Similar meetings were held in more than a thousand towns and cities east of the Mississippi River.

Christians who lived through that great movement of God said it was as if the Spirit of God was hovering over the Eastern seaboard. According to one account,

> Those on ships approaching the East Coast at times felt a solemn, holy influence even hundreds of miles from land. Revival began on one ship before it reached the coast. People on board began to feel the presence of God and a sense of their own sinfulness. The Holy Spirit convicted them and they began to pray. As the ship neared the harbor, the captain signaled, "Send a minister." Another commercial ship arrived in port with the captain, and every member of the crew converted in the last 150 miles of the journey. Ship after ship arrived in the ports of the East Coast with the same story. Passengers and crew were suddenly convicted of their sin and turned to Christ before they reached the American coast.[3]

What Christian does not long to experience such a gracious work of the Holy Spirit in his or her lifetime? Imagine a DC-10 full of passengers sensing the presence of Almighty God and coming under the conviction of sin. Imagine them crying out to God to be saved. Imagine the request coming over the airwaves to the air traffic controllers: "Send a minister!" Then imagine the man boarding the aircraft on the runaway in order to preach the life-saving gospel of Jesus Christ.

Or imagine what it would be like if revival came to your own congregation. Just imagine it! Imagine the church full on a weeknight, with people coming simply to pray. Imagine the leaders of the church openly confessing their sins. Imagine long-standing grudges settled in a moment through the reconciling grace of the Holy Spirit. Imagine teenagers coming forward to give their lives to Jesus Christ and to commit themselves to a lifetime of Christian service. And imagine members of the church in far distant places—missionaries, perhaps—being visited by the Spirit of God at the same moment.

God can do all that, and much, much more. We should long for him to do great and marvelous things in our times. Not that we can make God come in the power of the Holy Spirit. We cannot predict when he will come or even whether he will come. But there is one thing we can do, and that is to ask God to come. In his wonderful little book, *Prayer*, the Norwegian theologian O. Hallesby (1879–1961) writes, "We long for revivals; we speak of revivals; we work for revivals; and we even pray a little for them. But we do not enter upon that labor in prayer which is the essential preparation for every revival."[4]

If we want to see revival in our times we must pray, for it is God's usual method to send his reviving Spirit in response to the prayers of his people. Therefore revival ought to be one of the regular themes of every Christian's prayer life. Indeed, one of the surest signs that revival is needed is when prayer ceases to be a vital part of the life of a church or of an individual Christian.

Pray for revival. Start by kneeling in your prayer closet, drawing a circle around you, and asking God to revive everyone inside the circle. Then put revival on the prayer list for your small group. Ask God to revive your church, starting with the minister and working all the way to the smallest child. After that, ask God to revive the other churches in your city and even throughout the nation.

As we pray for the Holy Spirit to come and revive the church, we should pray in all humility, holding on to the promise God made through his prophet Isaiah:

> This is what the high and lofty One says—
>   he who lives forever, whose name is holy:
> "I live in a high and holy place,
>   but also with him who is contrite and lowly in spirit,
> to revive the spirit of the lowly
>   and to revive the heart of the contrite." (Isa. 57:15)

59

THE CHURCH IN THE POSTMODERN WORLD

*D*o you know what postmodernism is? If not, then you're not alone. A recent catalogue from Oxford publisher Basil Blackwell listed a dozen books on either modernity or postmodernity or both. There were books about postmodern ethics, postmodern philosophy, postmodern politics, postmodern aesthetics, and postmodern social theory.

Yet there seemed to be little consensus about whether modernism is coming or going, at Oxford or anywhere else. On the same page of the catalogue were two books entitled *The End of Modernity* and *The Persistence of Modernity*. Other writers want to have it *both* ways, as in a book called *The New Constellation: The Ethical-Political Horizons of Modernity/Postmodernity*.

Another scholar has written a sort of exposé on postmodernism, entitled *The Truth about Postmodernism*. There is even a book called *Modernity and Ambivalence*, but who cares?

Even those who can't agree about what postmodernism is can agree about this: it is the quest for something after modernism. It reveals the hunger in the human soul for Something Else. The postmodern looks at the modern world and says, "Is that all? Isn't there something else? Isn't there something more?" Postmodernism is the expression of the hope that modernism is dead. Hence its name: *postmodernism*.

What was the essential characteristic of modernism? It was this: human reason took the place of God in the modern world. So humanity turned to science, economics, and military power to solve its problems and to remake society. Modernism was a celebration of humanistic individualism. It was the attempt to live in a world ruled by man rather than God.

That world proved to be inhospitable. Some experts date the end of modernism and the beginning of postmodernism down to the minute. At 3:32 p.m. on July 15, 1972, the Pruitt-Igoe housing development in St. Louis was blown sky-high.[1] Pruitt-Igoe was a monument to modernity. It was a prize-winning piece of architecture, featuring the latest in modern technology, aesthetics, and design. It had everything that human reason could offer, but it turned out to be antihuman, impersonal, crime-ridden, and uninhabitable. It could not even be made safe but had to be blown out of its misery.

When people speak about postmodernism they sometimes mean ultramodern, modernity taken to the nth degree, what Zygmunt Bauman has termed "modernity without illusions." Postmodernism in this sense is not the replacement of modernism with something else, but modernism taken to its illogical extreme, a worldview built out of the rubble of modernism, not constructed from new materials.

But there is something new about postmodernism: its core belief that there are no absolutes. Like modernism, postmodernism throws out God, but it also throws out human rationality. Without God, modernism was characterized by moral relativism, a chaos of ethical values. Without reason, postmodernism is characterized by intellectual relativism, a chaos of mind. Postmodernism is not just moral relativism. It's much worse than that—it's absolute relativism, a relativism of truth. What may be true for you isn't true for me. Modernism replaced God with human reason; now postmodernism replaces human reason with raw feeling.

Living in the postmodern world as we do, it should not surprise us to discover that at least two-thirds of American adults do not believe in absolute truth. But it's worth considering for a moment how absurd, how nonsensical, how self-contradictory the core belief of postmodernism is. Postmoderns believe that there is no truth, which means that they do hold to at least one truth: the truth that there is no truth. Postmoderns believe that there are no absolutes, but the very belief that there are no absolutes is itself an absolute. The only absolute is relativism.

That makes postmodernism every bit as bankrupt as modernism—morally, spiritually, intellectually, socially, and architecturally. Postmodernism is hollow, an empty shell. Making up one's own truth is an empty enterprise. This is why I suspect that postmodernism won't be with us very long before we will be back to the same old questions: "Is that all? Isn't there something else? Isn't there something more?"

In the meantime, the church will have to live and witness in an increasingly postmodern culture, a culture without absolutes. In such a culture, what's okay for you is not okay for me and what's true for you may not be true for me. In such a culture, when we share our faith, people will say, "Isn't that nice for you?" People will be suspicious because we say that what's true is true, not only for me, but also for you. As believers in the absolute truth of Jesus Christ, we will have to live and witness in a culture that will make us ask again and again the question that David asked: "When the foundations are being destroyed, what can the righteous do?" (Ps. 11:3).

When the foundations are being destroyed, what *can* the righteous do? We give the same answer that David gave. "In the LORD I take refuge," he wrote (Ps. 11:1). "The LORD is in his holy temple; the LORD is on his heavenly throne. He observes the sons of men; his eyes examine them" (Ps. 11:4).

This isn't all there is. There is something else, something more. People may say that there are no absolutes, that there is no God and no truth, but it is God who scrutinizes and judges us, and not the other way around. This is our comfort when the foundations are being destroyed, when we witness the fragmentation and collapse of our culture, when we fear that there is nothing we can do. And this is the comfort we offer to those who are emptied and bruised by the postmodern world. The Lord is our refuge, he is on his heavenly throne, ruling and governing the world, and his rule is absolute.

60

THE POSTMODERN WORLD IN THE CHURCH

*P*ostmodernism is hard to pin down. Even most scholars have trouble defining the postmodern worldview. But modernism seems to be dying and we are living in an increasingly postmodern culture. What is new about postmodernism is the idea that there are no absolutes. Postmodernism isn't just moral relativism, like modernism, but intellectual relativism, a chaos of mind. Postmodernism throws out God, just like modernism did, but it also throws out human reason.

This is why postmodernism has such a negative tone. It sets itself against God, against reason, and against any coherent view of the world. The postmodernist says there is no such thing as absolute truth.

Something may be true for you, but it isn't necessarily true for me. If God is true for you, that's great, but he's not true for me. Marriage may be true for you, but it's not true for me. You may believe that there is an inherent difference between masculine and feminine, but that's not true for me.

Two-thirds of American adults say they do not believe that there is any absolute truth. Whenever someone says, "That may be true for you, but it's not true for me," we are staring into the face of postmodernism.

Postmodernism offers a giant smorgasbord of ideas, values, truths, impulses, and feelings, and then lets us choose whatever we want, as long as we don't try to force it on anyone else. In a way, postmodernism is at work in our homes. Anyone who has cable television with a remote control holds the controls to the postmodern world. Cable television is a giant smorgasbord of images, ideas, and impulses jumbled together. We can choose whatever we want. Plus we never have to follow any single story from beginning to end. We can check to see if the Bears are still beating the Redskins, and then "click," we can see what the weather is going to be like tomorrow, and then "click," we can watch a few minutes of a sitcom. Someone with a good sense of timing can keep track of two movies, three baseball games, and four shopping networks all at once. The networks are offering more and more programming for people who are incapable of following a single idea for more than thirty or forty seconds, bombarding viewers with a rapid series of images.

We find the same restlessness and shortness of attention span in the church. Various examples of Christian postmodernism were identified in an article in *The Christian Century* entitled "*Postconservative Evangelicals Greet the Postmodern Age.*"[1] These so-called postconservative evangelicals are not from the mainline seminaries and churches that ceased to be evangelical many years ago. No, these postconservatives consider themselves part of the evangelical community in the American church. What do they say about the proper source for Christian theology? Where do we get our doctrine?

Postconservatives seek to broaden the *sources* used in theology. . . . According to [them] . . . the essence of evangelicalism is an *experience* and a distinctive spirituality centered around it. . . . The essence of both Christianity and theology, then, is not . . . truths enshrined in doctrines, but a story-shaped experience. . . . [Theology] aids experience and doxology. In this servant task, theology draws on several sources. . . . These sources include the Bible, the tradition of Christian thought, culture (including philosophy, science and the arts), and the contemporary experience of God's community, including popular religion.[2]

Postconservative theology is theology with a remote control. We can listen to the Bible for a few minutes, and then "click," switch over to popular religion. We can listen to what contemporary science is saying for a little while, and then "click," consult the tradition of the church, before listening to our own spiritual experience, and that's how we arrive at theological truth.

There used to be a shorter word for postconservative evangelicalism. It was called liberalism. Remember liberal theology? Liberal theology rejected the Bible as the unique basis, the ultimate standard, and the only sufficient source for proper theology. It also incorporated culture and religious experience into Christian doctrine. Postconservative evangelicals are up to some of the same old tricks. The chaplain at Duke University, a mainline pastor from within the liberal tradition, recently surveyed the preaching landscape in evangelical churches. It all sounded so familiar to him that he called his article on the subject "Been There, Preached That."[3]

The best antidote for postmodernism in the church—for postconservative evangelicalism—is expository preaching. Expository preaching has seemed radical almost everywhere it has ever been introduced. Ezra the priest was an expository preacher. He read the law of God in Jerusalem after the children of Israel returned from exile in Babylon. As he read the law, he explained it so the people could understand it, and they wept with sorrow for their sins. Ulrich Zwingli (1484–1531) was an expository preacher, too. When the great Swiss Reformer started preaching at the Gross Münster in Zurich, he created quite a stir. One man was so electrified that he said he felt as if he had been seized by the hair and lifted from his pew. What was so electrifying? Zwingli had started at the beginning of Matthew's Gospel and preached through it a chapter at a time, verse by verse.

In a postmodern culture, expository preaching is becoming radical once again. When we open up our Bibles to hear the preaching of God's Word, we are asserting that there is a God who has the right to tell us what we need to hear. We are asserting that there is a single, authoritative standard for truth. We are asserting that the Bible is a coherent book that can profitably be read and studied in the order it has been given. We are asserting that God has an orderly mind and that it is worth our time to follow his ideas through from beginning to end. Over against all that is postmodern, we are asserting that there is such a thing as Truth, and that the Bible is where it can be found.

Notes

Introduction

1 This history is traced in Philip Graham Ryken, *Thomas Boston as Preacher of the Fourfold State*, Rutherford Studies in Historical Theology (Carlisle, UK: Paternoster, 1999).

Part 1: Christians in the World

1 Hans Rookmaaker, *Modern Art and the Death of a Culture* (Wheaton, Ill.: Crossway, 1994), 38.

Chapter 1: Inward Christian Soldiers

1 Paul Weyrich, "Moral Minority," *Christianity Today*, September 6, 1999, 44–45.

Chapter 2: The Accidental Evangelist

1 Statistics cited by Geoffrey L. Dennis in *Share the Good News*, October/November 1999, a newsletter produced by Good News Publishers.

2 Interview in *Pulse*, December 17, 1999, 5.

Chapter 6: The Wannamaker Name

1 This and other quotes and biographical information in this chapter are from William Allen Zulker, *John Wanamaker: King of Merchants* (Wayne, Pa.: Eaglecrest, 1993).

Chapter 8: Dead Sea Scrolls at Fifty

1 For a good overview of the subject, see Geza Vermes, *The Dead Sea Scrolls* (Philadelphia: Fortress, 1977).
2 The controversy is summarized in Kevin D. Miller, "The War of the Scrolls," *Christianity Today*, October 6, 1997, 38–45.
3 Millar Burrows, *The Dead Sea Scrolls* (New York: Viking, 1955), 320.
4 Westminster Confession of Faith, I.viii.
5 Peter Flint, *The Dead Sea Psalms Scrolls* (Leiden: E. J. Brill, 1997).

Chapter 9: Treasures in the Sand

1 In Michael A. Clark, *Focus*, autumn 1994.
2 Information in the preceding paragraphs comes from Michael D. Lemonick, "Are the Bible's Stories True?" *Time*, December 18, 1995, 62–70.

Chapter 10: The Stealth Bible

1 "The Stealth Bible," *World*, March 29, 1997, 12–15.
2 Timothy C. Morgan, "Biblical feminists press for gender-inclusive NIV," *Christianity Today*, September 1, 1997, 78.

Chapter 11: The Jesus Seminar

1 Robert W. Funk, Roy W. Hoover, and the Jesus Seminar, eds., *The Five Gospels: The Search for the Authentic Words of Jesus* (New York: Macmillan, 1993). For helpful reviews of *The Five Gospels*, see C. Stephen Evans, "Can the New Jesus Save Us?" *Books and Culture*, November/December 1995, 3–8; Richard B. Hays, "The Corrected Jesus," *First Things*, May 1994, 43–48; and Ben Witherington III, *The Jesus Quest* (Downers Grove, Ill.: InterVarsity Press, 1995).

Chapter 12: The New Harlequin Romance

1 David Blankenhorn, "Harlequin: Fathers to the Rescue," *Propositions* 6 (fall 1999):1–2.

Chapter 13: Adam Has Two Daddies

1 Details about Adam Holden Gallucio come from articles in the *Philadelphia Inquirer*.
2 In *At the Podium*, March 12, 1997, 3.

Chapter 14: No Surrender

1 Laura Doyle, *The Surrendered Wife: A Practical Guide to Finding Intimacy, Passion, and Peace with a Man* (New York: Simon and Schuster, 2001).

2 Ibid., 19–20.

Chapter 16: Fatherless America

1 See Thom S. Rainer, *The Bridger Generation* (Nashville: Broadman and Holman, 1997).

2 Ibid., 11.

3 Ibid., 29.

4 Ibid., 30.

5 Data from the Presbyterian Church in America, Atlanta, Georgia.

Chapter 17: Growing Kids the Ezzo Way

1 Gary Ezzo and Anne Marie Ezzo, *On Becoming Babywise,* (Sisters, Ore.: Questar, 1995).

2 Gary Ezzo and Anne Marie Ezzo, *Growing Kids God's Way: Biblical Ethics for Parenting,* 4th ed. (Chatsworth, Calif.: Growing Families International, 1993), 15.

Chapter 18: SCM Seeks SCF for LTR

1 Paige Benton, "Singled Out by God for Good," *Regeneration Quarterly* 3, no. 3, (1997): 20–21.

Chapter 21: The Serious Business of Heaven

1 C. S. Lewis, *Letters to Malcolm: Chiefly on Prayer* (London: Geoffrey Bles, 1963), 122.

2 This quotation and other biographical information in this essay come primarily from Maurice J. E. Brown, "Franz Peter Schubert," *The New Grove Dictionary of Music and Musicians,* ed. Stanley Sadie, 20 vols. (London: Macmillan, 1980), 16:752–811. For this chapter the help of Dr. Samuel Hsu, professor of music at Philadelphia Biblical University and an elder at Tenth Presbyterian Church, has been invaluable.

3 Ludwig van Beethoven, quoted in Brown, 767.

Chapter 22: Thanks for Mendelssohn

1 In R. Larry Todd, ed., *Mendelssohn and His World* (Princeton, N.J.: Princeton University Press, 1991), 311.

2 I am thankful for the kind assistance of Robert Carwithen and Samuel Hsu. For fur-

ther reading, Dr. Hsu recommends Eric Werner, *Mendelssohn: A New Image of the Composer and His Age* (Greenwood, S.C.: Attic Press, 1978). *Mendelssohn: A Life in Letters,* edited by Rudolf Elvers (New York: Fromm, 1990), gives a good sense of the composer's life and character. It is difficult to find critical work on Mendelssohn that does justice to the Christian dimension of his art. One of the most satisfying overviews of his musicianship is Todd's *Mendelssohn and His World.*

Chapter 23: Cézanne

1 Edmund Burke Feldman, *Varieties of Visual Experience,* 2d ed. (Englewood Cliffs, N.J.: Prentice-Hall, 1981), 315.

Chapter 24: Face to Face: Van Gogh's Portraiture

1 Quotations come from the letters of Vincent Van Gogh, as presented in audio and visual materials provided by the Philadelphia Museum of Art. See also Kathleen Erickson's articles in *Christianity and the Arts* 7, no. 3 (summer 2000).

Chapter 26: The Reverend Mr. Brocklehurst

1 The dialogue has been reconstructed from the text of Charlotte Brontë's *Jane Eyre* (New York: Barnes & Noble, 1993), 27.
2 Ibid., v.

Chapter 27: Evolution as Religion

1 Richard John Neuhaus, "The Public Square," *First Things,* February 1998, 75.
2 Richard Lewontin, *New York Review of Books,* (January 9, 1997), quoted in Phillip E. Johnson, "The Unraveling of Scientific Materialism," *First Things,* November 1997, 22–25.
3 Michael J. Behe, *Darwin's Black Box: The Biochemical Challenge to Evolution* (New York: Free Press, 1997).
4 See Phillip E. Johnson, "The Unraveling of Scientific Materialism," *First Things,* November 1997, 22–25.
5 Stephen Master, a doctor and researcher at the University of Pennsylvania, helped to clarify a number of points made in this essay.

Chapter 28: Cell Division

1 Michael Kinsley, *Time,* June 25, 2001, 80.

Chapter 29: Take Two Prayers and Call Me in the Morning

1 The information in this chapter comes from David B. Larson and Susan S. Larson, "The Forgotten Factor in Physical and Mental Health—What Does the Research Show?" (Washington, D.C.: National Institutes for Healthcare Research, 1994).

Chapter 30: Homo Sapiens for Sale

1 Mark Derry, *Escape Velocity* (NY: Grove, 1996).
2 Marvin Minsky, Massachusetts Institute of Technology, quoted in "Preparing for the Brave Millennium," *Christianity Today*, December 7, 1998, 34.

Chapter 31: Earth Day

1 E. O. Wilson, "Earth Day 2000," *Time*, Spring 2000 Special Issue: "Vanishing Before Our Eyes," vol. 155, no. 17, 29–33.

Chapter 32: Digital Angel

1 Information on and analysis of the Digital Angel comes from John W. Whitehead's "On Target" column in the winter 2000 edition of a newsletter from The Rutherford Institute.

Chapter 34: Ashkelon in America

1 Archaeological details come from Lawrence Stager and Patricia Smith, "DNA Analysis Sheds New Light on Oldest Profession at Ashkelon," *Biblical Archaeology Review* 23, no. 4 (July/August 1997): 16.
2 Papyrus Oxyrhynchus 744, in Naphtali Lewis, *Life in Egypt under Roman Rule* (Oxford: Oxford University Press, 1985), 54.
3 Greg Koukl, "Arguments for the Humanness of a Fetus," *Journal of Christian Apologetics* 1, no. 1 (summer 1997): 89–114.

Chapter 35: The Massacre of the Innocents

1 See Madeleine L'Engle, *The Glorious Impossible* (New York: Simon and Schuster, 1990).

Chapter 36: The Lust of the Eyes

1 Associated Press, March 1, 2000.
2 Harry W. Schaumburg, *False Intimacy*, rev. ed. (Colorado Springs, Colo.: NavPress, 1997), 23.

Chapter 38: Not Worth the Gamble

1 For information on the report, see the *Philadelphia Inquirer*, March 27, 1996, A1.
2 Margot Hornblower, "No Dice," *Time*, April 1, 1996, 29–33.
3 Tertullian, *De Spectaculis (The Shows)*, xv, quoted in David H. Field, "Gambling," in David J. Atkinson etal., *New Dictionary of Christian Ethics and Pastoral Theology* (Downers Grove, IL: InterVarsity, 1995), 402.
4 Westminster Larger Catechism (1647), Q & A 142.
5 These principles are drawn from William Temple (1881–1944), *Essays in Christian Politics and Kindred Subjects* (London: Longmans Green, 1927).
6 Jeremy Taylor, "Sermon on the Cards," quoted in Field, 402.

Chapter 39: Road Rage

1 *Philadelphia Inquirer*, February 19, 1998, A4.
2 David Engwicht, *Reclaiming Our Cities and Towns: Better Living with Less Traffic* (Philadelphia: New Society, 1993).

Chapter 40: Cheaters Never Prosper

1 National survey data come from the *Philadelphia Inquirer*, 1997.

Chapter 41: That Demon, Sport

1 Roger Angell, *The Summer Game* (New York: Penguin, 1972), 291–92.

Chapter 43: I Was in Prison

1 Quotes and statistics come from Don Smarto, ed., *Setting the Captives Free* (Grand Rapids, Mich.: Baker, 1993), and from ministry literature provided by Prison Fellowship.

Chapter 44: Talking Turkey

1 *Journals of Congress*, November 1777, 854–55.
2 George Washington, quoted in *PCA Messenger*, November 1993, 6.

Chapter 46: The True Meaning of Christmas

1 *Directory for the Publick Worship of God*, "An Appendix."
2 C. S. Lewis, *Letters to an American Lady*, December 29, 1958 (Grand Rapids, MI: Eerdmans, 1967), 77.
3 B. B. Warfield, *Four Hymns and Some Religious Verses* (Philadelphia: Westminster, 1910).

Chapter 47: I Shop, Therefore I Am

1 James Twitchell, *Lead Us into Temptation: The Triumph of American Materialism* (New York: Columbia University Press, 1999).

2 Mark Buchanan, "Trapped in the Cult of the Next Thing," *Christianity Today,* September 6, 1999, 63–72.

Chapter 48: The Trouble with Santa

1 Penne L. Restad, *Christmas in America: A History* (New York: Oxford University Press, 1995), 45.

2 Ibid., 47–50; Restad shows where Moore derived the ideas for his poem.

3 Ibid., 51.

4 John Shlien, "Santa Claus: The Myth in America," *A Review of General Semantics* 16 (summer 1959): 398.

Chapter 49: As Far as the East Is from the West

1 For further details, consult Mark A. Noll, *Turning Points: Decisive Moments in the History of Christianity* (Grand Rapids, Mich.: Baker, 1997), or Kallistos Ware, *The Orthodox Way,* rev. ed. (Crestwood, N.Y.: St. Vladimir's Seminary Press, 1995).

2 Henry Bettenson, ed., *Documents of the Christian Church,* 2d ed. (New York: Oxford University Press, 1963), 97.

Chapter 50: On a Crusade

1 Reported in *Evangelicals Now,* February 1999.

2 Steven Runciman, *A History of the Crusades,* 3 vols. (New York: Cambridge University Press, 1954), 3:123.

Chapter 51: When Catholics Were Catholic

1 Thomas Aquinas, *Summa Theologiae: A Concise Translation,* ed. Timothy McDermott (London: Methuen, 1989), 173–74.

2 Ibid., 322.

3 Ibid., 323.

Chapter 52: Wycliffe, Bible Translator

1 Rheims Bible, in David Daniell, *William Tyndale: A Biography* (New Haven, Conn.: Yale University Press, 1994), 95.

Chapter 53: Bonfire of the Vanities

1 Biographical details come from the *Oxford Dictionary of Church History* and the *Oxford Encyclopedia of the Reformation.*

2 F. B. Meyer, *Jeremiah*, rev. ed. (Fort Washington, Pa.: Christian Literature Crusade, 1993), 107.

3 Pope Paul IV, quoted in William Robinson Clark, *Savonarola, His Life and Times* (Chicago: McClurg, 1890), 417.

Chapter 54: Consumer Report on Religion
1 Dietrich Bonhoeffer, *The Cost of Discipleship*, rev. ed. (New York, Macmillan, 1959), 99.

Chapter 55: A Short Theology of the Tulip
1 Leland Ryken et al., eds., *Dictionary of Biblical Imagery* (Downers Grove, Ill.: Inter-Varsity Press, 1999), 294.

2 For more information about the glorious tulip, see Anna Pavord, *The Tulip: The Story of a Flower That Has Made Men Mad* (London: Bloomsbury, 1999).

Chapter 56: The Place of Hell
1 David O'Reilly, "Anglican's Take on the Netherworld Stirs Fiery Debate," *Philadelphia Inquirer*, January 21, 1996, A19.

2 See D. P. Walker, *The Decline of Hell* (London: Routledge & Kegan Paul, 1964).

Chapter 57: The Coming Revival
1 Bill Bright, *The Coming Revival* (Orlando, Fla.: New Life Publications, 1995).

2 Dale Schlafer, *A Revival Primer* (Denver, Colo.: Promise Keepers, 1997).

3 Stephen Olford, *Heart Cry for Revival* (Grand Rapids, Mich.: Zondervan, 1969), quoted in Schlafer, 8.

4 D. Martyn Lloyd-Jones, *Revival* (Wheaton, Ill.: Crossway, 1987), quoted in Schlafer, 9.

5 Schlafer, *A Revival Primer*, 9–10.

Chapter 58: Praying for Revival
1 Calvin Colton, *The History and Character of American Revivals of Religion* (London: F. Westley and A. H. Davis, 1832).

2 Asa Nettleton, quoted by Winkey Pratney, *Revival: Its Principles and Personalities* (Lafayette, Pa.: Huntington House, 1994), in Dale Schlafer, *A Revival Primer* (Denver, Colo.: Promise Keepers, 1997).

3 Wesley Duewel, *Revival Fire* (Grand Rapids, Mich.: Zondervan, 1995), quoted in Schlafer, 51–52.

4 O. Hallesby, *Prayer*, trans. Clarence J. Carlsen (Minneapolis, Minn.: Augsburg, 1931), 75–76.

Chapter 59: The Church in the Postmodern World

1 Charles Jencks, in Gene Edward Veith Jr., *Postmodern Times* (Wheaton, Ill.: Cross-way, 1994), 39.

Chapter 60: The Postmodern World in the Church

1 Roger E. Olson, "*Post*conservative Evangelicals Greet the *Post*modern Age," *The Christian Century*, May 3, 1995, 480–83.

2 Ibid., 481.

3 William Willimon, "Been There, Preached That," *Leadership* 16, no. 4 (1995): 74–78.

Index of Persons

Index of Scripture